Pet Clean-Up Made Easy

PET
CLEAN-UP
MADE EASY

by Don Aslett

Illustrated by
Robert L. Betty

Writer's Digest Books, Cincinnati, Ohio

Pet Cleanup Made Easy. Copyright © 1988 by Don A. Aslett. Printed and bound in the United States of America. All rights reserved. No part of this book may be reproduced in any form or by any electronic or mechanical means including information storage and retrieval systems without permission in writing from the publisher, except by a reviewer, who may quote brief passages in a review. Published by Writer's Digest Books, an imprint of F&W Publications, Inc., 1507 Dana Avenue, Cincinnati, Ohio 45207. First edition.

93 92 91 90 89 88   5 4 3 2

Library of Congress Cataloging-in-Publication Data

Aslett, Don, 1935-
  Pet cleanup made easy.
  Includes index.
  1. Dogs—Cleaning. 2. Cats—Cleaning. 3. Pet cleanup. 4. House cleaning. I. Title.
SF427.48.A75   1988   636.08'87   88-224
ISBN 0-89879-262-2

Design by Craig LaGory
A White Oak Edition

Acknowledgments

This book would not have been possible without the help of a number of top professionals in a variety of related fields. These people demonstrated over and over that expert knowledge and deep concern for the safety and welfare of animals everywhere will overcome even self-interest, commercial rivalry, and the chronic lack of time in the modern world.

Micky Niego, Companion Animal Services counselor of the New York City ASPCA and professional dog trainer, brought us ingenious and down-to-earth answers to a great many of our pet paradoxes, expressed in unmistakable style.

Gwen Bohnenkamp, of the Animal Behavior Department of the San Francisco SPCA, and *Ian Dunbar* of the Center for Applied Animal Behavior, provided unusually readable and helpful pamphlets on a great variety of pet problem subjects.

Shirlee Kalstone, professional groomer and author, added important inside knowledge to the sections on Bathing and Grooming.

Nicki Meyer, of the Nicki Meyer Educational Effort, "America's pet crate expert," helped us see that this important topic was not neglected.

Dr. Jane Bicks, animal nutritionist and author, answered all those "one more questions" with grace and flair.

Boris Tatistcheff, of Gem State Pest Control, Inc., filled in any last gaps in my knowledge of fleas.

Dian Dincin Buchman helped with early brainstorming on the book.

Larry Andrews shared his very special knowledge of, and feeling for, cats and dogs.

Fancy Publications (*Cat Fancy, Dog Fancy,* and *Bird Talk,* especially *Kathy Thornton*) provided a wealth of very much to the point wisdom.

Cats Magazine.

Dr. Larry C. Mitchell of the Utah Veterinary Medical Association Lay Education Committee.

Dr. Peggy Harrer, of Community Animal Hospital, Pocatello, and *Dr. Christine Teets* of Animal Medical Center, Idaho Falls.

Dr. Marjorie L. Smith and *Dr. Edna Guibor* of Smith-Sager Publications.

The Humane Society of the United States (especially *Barbara Cassidy*).

The Bide-A-Wee Home Association (especially *Debbie Feliziani*).

Save Our Strays (especially *Bea Sellers*).

The Closter Animal Welfare Society of Closter, New Jersey, formerly Lost Pet Service, Inc. (especially **Joan Keating**).

The American Kennel Club (especially **John Mandeville** and the American Kennel Club *Gazette*).

The Purdue University Veterinary Medical Library (especially **Gretchen Stephens**).

Cornell University College of Agriculture and Life Science.

The University of Idaho—Cooperative Extension Service.

The American Veterinary Medical Association.

The California Veterinary Medical Association.

Animal Care & Welfare, Inc. (SPCA) of Pittsburgh, Pennsylvania.

The Pet Information Bureau.

The Pet Industry Joint Advisory Council.

The Pets Are Wonderful Council.

Associated Humane Societies, Inc.

Friends of Animals, Inc.

The American Humane Association.

L. J. Bishop, Jr., of Clean Care Seminars.

The Association of Specialists in Cleaning and Restoration.

The National 4-H Council.

The Boy Scouts of America.

Consolidated Chemical Company (especially **Marvin Klein** and **Warren Weisberg**).

The Bramton Company (especially **Al Irons**).

Franklin Labs (especially **Lowell Grauberger** and **Dr. John Schnackel**).

Nilodor, Inc. (especially **Les Mitson** and **Hal Kehoe**).

Gaines Professional Services.

The Alpo Pet Center.

The Carnation Company.

The Ralston Purina Company.

Procter & Gamble.

Airchem Industries.

The Ryter Corporation (especially **Barb Nelson**).

Farnam Pet Products.

The Idaho State University and Cincinnati Public Libraries.

And the excellent books on pet care and training by **Mordecai Siegal** and **Matthew Margolis**, **Roger Caras**, **Dr. Michael Fox**, **Sara Stein**, and **Robert Allen** and **William Westbrook**, among many others.

TABLE OF CONTENTS

NOTE: For the sake of simplicity and ease of reading, when the sex of the animal is not relevant to the issue being discussed, pets are referred to in these pages with the pronouns "he" and "him."

INTRODUCTION

On the farm in Idaho where I grew up, we had a lot of animals, all of the outside variety. In addition to the cattle, hogs, horses, and other livestock we raised, we always had an assortment of dogs and cats. On a farm, every creature is expected to pay its own way, and the dogs and cats each had responsibilities as watchdog, cattle herder, or mouser.

This is how I happened to come to love and appreciate animals, and it wasn't until I left the farm and became a professional cleaner—and married, and had six children—that I discovered the very different world of animals kept as pets in homes. I suddenly realized that urban and suburban animal owners were faced with problems we simply didn't have in a rural setting. People and their pets live so closely together today in today's smaller homes, apartments, and condos that some of the most puzzling and discouraging housework jobs have to do with pets. And in thirty years of professional cleaning I've seen firsthand how many people are frustrated because they love their animals but don't know how to deal with the cleaning problems they bring.

Although I touched on a few aspects of pet cleaning in my three previous best-sellers *(Is There Life After Housework?, Do I Dust or Vacuum First?,* and *Clutter's Last Stand),* I never really delved into the problems. And at the height of my career, as I was becoming known as America's #1 Cleaning Expert, I realized that few people, if any (not even all of my fellow professionals) truly knew how to deal with all the problems of cleaning up after and around pets. In the houses, apartments, offices, and public buildings I cleaned, and in the radio and TV appearances I made as a cleaning professional who wrote books, people kept asking hard and pressing questions about pet food mess, litter, shedding, spraying, pet stains, and of course, *odor.* In letters, calls, and in person, the pleas were the same: how do we make pet cleanup easier and more effective?

When I set about finding the answers to all the tough questions pet owners asked, I found that the knowledge was scattered and contradictory, or outdated old wives' tales, or nobody had ever thought about it from a cleaning angle. Some of the "cures" seemed worse than the disease, in terms of the mess they'd make.

Pet cleaning was clearly a neglected area.

So I sought out and combined the knowledge of professional cleaners and scientists, pet doctors, pet products manufacturers, individual pet owners, pet organizations, and publications (books and magazines, popular and technical)—and tried to put it all together in a way that pet owners young and old could understand and use.

You will learn, in these pages, how to clean up the mess better and faster—and also how to *prevent* it from ever happening in the first place. (Would you rather spend a couple of days teaching a dog with muddy paws to wait till you've wiped his feet off, and twenty minutes installing a mat—or the rest of your life wiping up muddy pawprints?)

Is there a pet that doesn't make any kind of ripple or dent in "House Beautiful"? There's no such animal. Anywhere there's life, action and enjoyment, there's going to be some mess. But pets also add a certain adventure to life, a feeling of anticipation, of "what's going to happen next?" You can always count on something to make houselife more exciting than the weekly dusting of the piano.

There's no question about it, animals kept inside will mean some extra work, and call for some extra precautions. But if you go about it right—as I hope to show you in this book—it won't be a major or endless undertaking. And it's well worth it, because in the ever more blacktop and concrete world of today we *need* pets around us more than ever before.

Owning pets doesn't have to drive us to the brink of insanity, or force us to abandon our standards of cleanliness and order. We can live happily and harmoniously with our pets if we just apply a little imagination and a little common sense and a little expert knowledge about proper procedures and equipment. That's the reason for this book, to enable us all to enjoy our pets without constant hassle and anxiety. My most sincere wish is that it helps *you* to that end.

Don Aslett

Don A. Aslett

America's #1 Cleaner

CHAPTER 1

Pet cleaning 101

No Pets or Children Allowed . . .

Signs like this bother me, because somewhere underneath is the assumption that a dirty, damaged home is synonymous with pet or child occupancy. We don't need to demand the banishment of furry friends or little humans simply because they require some extra cleaning measures and precautions. They may call for a few minor adjustments in our surroundings and lifestyle, but nothing worth having in life is entirely free and easy. But to make it as easy as possible, this book is meant to guide you through the *what, when, how,* and *why* of pet cleaning.

The three most important ingredients of success in real estate, in order, are: location, location, location. And believe it or not, it's about the same for the happy and healthy ownership of pets: *A Place, a Place, a Place.*

A PLACE IN OUR LIFE
This means *time,* to play with our pets and to exercise them, to train them, to love, groom, and clean up after them.

A PLACE IN OUR HOME
Pets aren't an afterthought that can fit in anywhere—we have to give them the space and liberty to live and move.

A PLACE IN OUR BUDGET
You can bet that part of the twelve billion dollars being spent each year in the U.S. on pets is going to be our cash—for food, vet bills, vaccinations, licenses, accessories. It doesn't have to cost a lot of money to own a pet, but some things are a lot more important than others—such as the right kind of pet food and shelter, and the right kind of cleaning supplies.

When we take pet ownership upon ourselves, we accept the responsibility of keeping our animals safe and clean and well cared for, of providing them with the conditions conducive to a happy and healthy life. And if we give them the facilities they need, and the proper training and encouragement, most pets will do a lot to help keep *themselves* clean and neat.

If You Leave, You Grieve

Timing and tools are the main differences between "pet cleaning" and plain old housecleaning.

You can't let pet mess go until it's convenient, because if you leave it, the mess will spread, stain, smell, attract pests, and encourage repeat offenses.

Spills and "accidents" rarely stain if cleaned up while the mess is still fresh and moist or new. But give them a

chance to lie there, and you'll often have permanent damage to fabrics and finishes and furnishings.

Also, odors penetrate deeper and grow more offensive the longer they're left. Germs multiply and many disease spores and parasite eggs reach the infective stage after the mess has been left awhile. Clean it up sooner and it's a lot safer.

Four Simple Steps to Most Pet Cleaning

Food slops and spills, sticky pawprints, many a smear or streak might appear stubborn and here to stay. But softening the mark or material is all you basically need to do, to bring it back to its original entirely removable liquid state. What the smudge consists of will determine the solution you need to work with; grease, oil, or tar call for solvent or spot remover, but all-purpose cleaning solution is fine for most other things.

These basic principles apply to almost every cleanable, hard-surface item. (The exceptions are soft porous materials like fabric, leather, and unfinished wood—cleaning these is tougher.) Pet stuff with a smooth hard

3

surface always means faster and easier cleaning.

1. Remove: *Before you clean or wash anything, remember that just as it makes sense to sweep a floor before you mop it, it only takes a second to remove the bulk of the dirt—scrape it off, brush it off, or knock it off—first. This is one of the most important principles of cleaning, yet we so often fail to follow it. If the material has dried into a thick hard crust, scrape off what you can with a razor blade or putty knife before wetting the spot. Be careful here. You're only trying to dislodge the bulk of the deposit before you move on to*

2. Spray or dampen *the article liberally with the cleaning solution. All-purpose cleaning solution, or dish detergent and water, will do fine for most general-purpose pet cleaning.*

3. Let it soak: *Give the solution two to five minutes to work, depending on how tough a job you're tackling. This will give the "surfactant" in the cleaner time to pull the dirt and grease from the surface and suspend them in the cleaning solution. Pro cleaners call this emulsifying the enemy!*

This approach works 95 percent of the time. Once the smudge is softened, you can just wipe it off. Any article that's waterproof, such as rubber bones or plastic food dishes, can be soaked overnight in cleaning solution. Then those tough deposits will wipe right off with little effort.

4. Wipe or rinse: *No matter how good the thing looks after you've removed and dampened and soaked, there's still a residue of soap and dissolved goo on there (as well as chemical traces from your cleaning solution that could harm pets, if they come in*

contact with it.) Rinsing well with clear water is best—if for some reason that's just not possible, wipe the surface thoroughly with a piece of clean terry toweling dampened in clean water.

Important Tools and Techniques for the Pet Cleaner

In pet cleaning, even more so than in regular cleaning, the right tools and supplies are important to your ability to do a fast and effective job. When it comes to "chemicals" you want something designed and tested to be safe for and around pets. That's why it's usually better to get them from a reputable pet store, pet supply catalog, or veterinarian rather than a supermarket or discount store. The personnel in such places will also be better equipped to answer any questions you may have. Buy a product made specifically for the animal you have in mind. Never use cat shampoo on dogs, dog flea spray on cats, etc. All of these things are specially formulated for a specific animal's skin and coat and chemical tolerances. Certain chemicals kill cats but don't harm dogs, for example. Even the age of the pet involved can make a difference. Manufacturers print specific instructions and warnings on the label as to how the product should be used. Make it a point to *read* that fine print on the label.

Professional-quality tools and supplies, though available in pet supply and janitorial supply stores and specialty mail order catalogs, aren't easy to come by in every part of the country. So many of the following items—some of the most widely useful ones for pet purposes—can be ordered from Housework, Inc., P.O. Box 39, Pocatello, ID 83204.

SQUEEGEE

This is the undiscovered pet cleaning tool that cleans all kinds of spills and messes—liquid, solid, or unpleasantly in between—off all kinds of surfaces, swiftly and sanitarily. And a squeegee is the professional way to clean windows—and the outside of fishtanks—quickly and without leaving streaks. Ettore Steccone is a good professional-quality brand; use the 6-inch size for general pet cleanup and the 10-inch size (or larger) for windows.

The squeegee's rubber blade will sweep up wet, mushy, or dry messes on carpet, concrete, or couches in seconds, leaving only a light film to be wiped up or otherwise dealt with. And then you can use it again (only now you want a floor squeegee) after cleaning to swiftly remove the rinse water from the area. The brass and rubber of a good squeegee are chemically inert, so they're resistant to the acids, alkalies, and protein compounds so often involved in pet cleaning. Pet messes won't penetrate or be absorbed by the blade, nor can they hurt it in any way.

DUSTPAN

A dustpan has 101 uses, especially in pet cleanup jobs. It's the perfect companion to your all-purpose 6-inch squeegee, for getting up pet messes fast. You want a dustpan that really fits flush to the floor, is easy to wash and rinse, and won't rust. An industrial-strength molded rubber or plastic pan has a good deep well and a keen edge.

Use your dustpan and squeegee to clean up:

- *Food spills—the rubber blade slicks up both liquid and lumps in a second.*

- *Feces—let your dustpan and the squeegee do the dirty work to clean droppings off hard floors, rugs, or street surfaces.*

- *Vomit—get the bulk of it up and off hard flooring or carpet fast to prevent staining and smell penetration.*

- *A variety of other unpleasant pet problems—broken glass, mud, and even unidentifiable messes brought in by pets.*

A squeegee and dustpan can be washed and rinsed off in seconds, much easier than cleaning rags or brushes. Just slosh a dirty squeegee in a bucket of soapy water, or sponge or hose it off.

PROFESSIONAL-QUALITY PLASTIC BROOM

If you're using a broom with conventional "corn" bristles, the first stroke will move 85 percent of the dust or debris, the next stroke 10 percent of what remains, and a third stroke will get most of the remaining 5 percent. A split-bristle synthetic broom, on the other hand, will move 100 percent in just two strokes. I'm talking about the professional-quality plastic brooms such as the one made by Rubbermaid with an angled head and "split ends."

Pro brooms get in the corners easier, will last much longer, and won't shed like straw brooms. And they're easier to clean when they get soiled or stained.

(And if you want to sweep the way the pros do, here's a tip: Most people sweep too slowly; quick, short, downward strokes are the most efficient.)

DUST MOP

There's nothing better for whisking up hair, feathers, dust, or other pet fallout from any hard-surface floor. Professional dust mop treatment will keep your dust mop "sticky" enough to grab the dirt and dust and hold on to it. (Shake out or vacuum the mophead regularly; launder it when it gets dirty.)

NYLON-BACKED SCRUBBING SPONGE

A white nylon pad bonded to a sponge, such as the one made by 3M, for scrubbing off hard-to-remove soil safely. The white nylon won't scratch household surfaces the way the more abrasive green nylon pads often will.

PROFESSIONAL ALL-PURPOSE SCRUB BRUSH

For cleaning cages and litter pans, and any place in pet cleaning where real scrubbing is called for. The design of this brush eliminates skinned knuckles and the all-nylon bristles, bristle bed, and handle can't crack or wear out or be affected by hot water or strong cleaning solutions. It's 100 percent sanitary, rinses fast and dries quickly, and will outlast ordinary brushes.

PET RAKE

This is a hair remover that works! The stiff crimped nylon bristles of this tool do an amazing job of gathering hair, fur, lint, fuzz, and cobwebs off furniture, bedding, draperies, rugs, car interiors, even clothing. You can use it as is, or mount it on a long handle for a longer reach.

COMMERCIAL UPRIGHT VACUUM

This is your best friend, when it comes to pet cleaning. Be sure your vacuum has a beater bar or "power head" that will knock the dirt loose. If it doesn't, then hair and other light debris will

Pet rake

Professional all-purpose scrub brush

Carpet spot removal brush

Professional cleaning towel

cling, with the help of static electricity, to their original nesting place, regardless of how magnificent your vacuum is, or how strong its suction. *Loosened debris* is the secret of effective vacuuming—you have to get the dirt free of the carpet so it can join the air flow and end up in the bag. The beater bar bounces and vibrates the carpet to free hair, dander, dirt, and fleas, then the brushes sweep it into the flow of air and up into the vacuum bag.

This is also why you want a vacuum, not a carpet sweeper. Carpet sweepers just wisk off the surface litter. The carpet looks clean because the visible stuff is gone, but there's still dirt and grit down in the fibers that make your carpet wear out faster.

The best all-purpose vacuum for home use, in my opinion, is the Eureka C-2740, a 6-amp model with a 12-inch beater bar, a sturdy cloth bag, and a long cord. Don't bother to get the attachments for an upright; most of them are awkward to use and you lose 30-40 percent of your upright vacuum's pickup power when you add an attachment.

WET-DRY VACUUM

The beauty of a wet-dry is that it can suck in both dry debris and all kinds of liquids, at the quick and simple change of a filter. This means that urine, upchuck, spills, etc. on a carpet can be swooped up untouched by human hands, after you've used a squeegee and dustpan to pick up the worst of it.

For instance, you can use a wet-dry to clean concrete dog runs and other hard waterproof surfaces. It's a much better approach than just "hosing it off," which often leaves concrete surfaces, especially, wet and clammy. Wet the surface with your cleaning solution and scrub

A beater bar—shown here on an upright vacuum—is the secret to effective vacuuming.

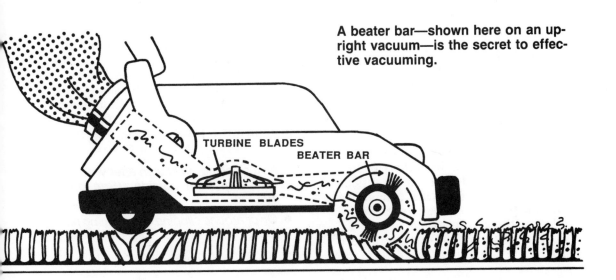

TURBINE BLADES BEATER BAR

with a stiff broom or nylon-bristle brush, then vacuum up the dirty solution. Then rinse and remove every trace of the rinse water with the wet-dry.

You can also use it for disinfecting hard surfaces or carpeting. After cleaning, apply your disinfecting solution (see page 25), let it sit ten minutes or so, and pick it back up with the wet-dry. Then rinse the area and use the wet-dry to pick up the rinse water.

Get a 5- or 6-gallon model with a rust-resistant metal or plastic tank and a side hose attachment. Here you do want some attachments: an upholstery attachment, a small brush head, a squeegee head, floor tool, and crevice tool. Five-gallon wet-drys run $39.95 to $89.95, or you can get a deluxe stainless steel commercial model for about $300.

A CORDLESS HAND VACUUM

is great for "wisp cleaning." You can pick up few stray blades of grass or straw, burrs, feathers, crumbs, or bits of gravel without arming yourself with the whole arsenal of broom, vacuum, and mop. The latest model of the Dustbuster (generally considered to be the superior species of these mini-vacs) even has a beater bar on it, to beat the dirt out of the carpet just like the bigger vacuums do. This enables it to do a good job even on that true test of pet cleaning—hair removal. The stiff bristles on the bar stand up the nap and loosen and pull the hair out.

PROFESSIONAL MATS

are a #1 priority in pet cleaning—pets aren't likely to wipe their own feet so you have to put something there to do it for them. The right kind of mats outside and inside of your doors is like having a full-time pet janitor-in-waiting. They'll collect and concentrate pet debris for easy cleaning, knock off dirt, and absorb moisture before it gets tracked into the

house. A 3x5-foot mat both inside and outside each door assures enough steps on the matting to do a good job of pulling off grit and loose litter. Use mats of nylon or olefin fiber on vinyl or rubber backing inside; outside mats of polypropylene artificial turf on vinyl or rubber backing are best.

Matting is also a great thing to install in other high pet use areas. Its soft nap provides a tempting place for a pet to lie down, and the matting will pull burrs, loose hairs, and dirt off the pet onto a surface that is easily cleaned. Nylon or olefin mats with rubber or vinyl backing are soft, warm, and absorbent, and they're also easily cleaned and disinfected. Mats are also portable and can be moved anywhere you need them—it's much easier to clean something that's movable like a mat than something that's permanently fixed. And mats are inexpensive enough to have extras and rotate their use. Use mats:

- *As a cleaning-off station after your dog comes in from outside. (See page 105.)*

- *On or around clipping or grooming platforms.*

- *Under the food and water dish.*

8

- *Inside and outside a pet door (the nylon or olefin type inside, artificial turf type outside), mats will scrape off every bit of trackable stuff.*

- *An artificial turf mat in front of animal dwellings outdoors will keep the inside of the doghouse cleaner. And inside the doghouse or other animal quarters, a nylon or olefin mat will provide a warm, waterproof bed.*

- *As a travel aid—a 2x3-foot nylon or olefin mat is a convenient and comfortable pet base for the back of any vehicle or the floor of the motel room, when you get there. The rubber or vinyl backing won't leak or rot, so if your pet does have an accident en route you're well covered.*

THE DISINFECTANT THAT'S SAFEST TO USE AROUND PETS

Chlorasan, made by Franklin Labs of Ft. Dodge, Iowa, is both the most effective of the commonly available disinfectants *and* the gentlest and least toxic. It's easy on household surfaces, pet equipment, and living quarters, as well as on human and animal skin. The very same product (Chlorhexidine diacetate) is sold through vets under the name Nolvasan; Chlorasan is what it's called when it's sold over the counter through feed or pet-supply stores. Use it to disinfect walls, floors, pet accessories, grooming tools, pet dishes, bedding— you name it. It can even be added to the laundry. (More on disinfectants on page 24.)

Pet Stain and Odor Removers

The main reason pet stains and odors are so hard to deal with is that these particular messes (urine, feces, vomit, etc.) are largely composed of "organic" materials which not only have strong odors, either initially or as they begin to decay, but also provide excellent fuel for subsequent bacteria and fungus growth that creates a second source of odor and stain.

You aren't likely to find products that will really do the tough job of removing pet stains and odors in ordinary department stores or supermarkets. These tough jobs call for some professional products formulated for this very purpose.

CHEMICAL DEODORIZER/CLEANERS

These are the specialized pet deodorizer/cleaners sold in pet shops and by vets, which are effective, safe odor neutralizers.

For cleaning pet accidents off nonporous hard surfaces, a chemical deodorizer is the best choice. (Many of these products have a cleaning agent built right into them, so they don't require an additional cleaning step.) You simply spray it on after you clean up the mess, and it does the job. For semiporous hard surfaces like flat wall paint, chemical deodorizers are still the best to use, although some products can't be used on plastic, paint, rayon, silk, or noncolorfast fabrics. It's always best to test any cleaning product you're unfamiliar with in an inconspicuous spot before using it overall, to make sure it won't damage or discolor the surface, and always be sure to follow the precautions on the label.

The chemical deodorizer/cleaners I prefer are Nilotex, from the Nilodor Company and Dog-Tex from the Consolidated Chemical Company of Chicago. They're widely available in pet stores and janitorial supply stores. Nilotex is safe to use on all colorfast fabrics that won't be damaged by water, and it's gentle enough for upholstery cleaning. Fresh 'N' Clean works well, too, but it leaves behind a perfumey fragrance that you may not care for. Products like these are great for cleaning up accidents on hard floors as well as for deodorizing pet living areas.

Another set of products I've had good success with are those from Robinson Labs: Urine & Stool Deodorizer and Pet Stain Remover. You use the deodorizer first to neutralize the odor, and then the stain remover to eliminate any remaining stains.

Odor and Damage— Where Is It?

It isn't always in a single puddle, that's for sure. Often when you find where Fido did it, you don't realize the carpet or corner isn't the whole story. To expand your "where to find it" vocabulary, consider this:

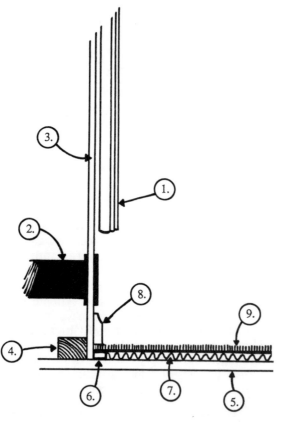

1. *Drapes and other fabric surfaces are porous and absorb odors.*
2. *Heat or air ducts (and their filters) can harbor odor because they move malodorous air through the house.*
3. *The sheet rock of the walls can absorb and hold accident odor and then release it later.*
4. *Pet mess moisture can even reach the very structure of the house— such as the wall studs—and stay.*
5. *The subfloor—generally plywood or pressboard—often has urine seeped all the way down into it.*
6. *The carpet tack strip is raw wood and sucks in anything moist.*
7. *The carpet pad is usually made of materials like urethane or foam rubber that grab and hold odor. And moisture or humidity will activate it forevermore.*
8. *Even the unfinished back of the baseboard can pick up and hold odor.*
9. *The carpet gets the bulk of the odor-producing organic substances from pet accidents—in the backing and the nap.*

You can see why a drop or two of magic deodorizer won't instantly eliminate a pet odor problem!

As a rule of thumb, the chemical deodorizer/cleaners work well on hard surfaces and may be all you need for your carpet, if you catch the stains quickly. But if you're dealing with old urine stains, or repeated sieges of vomiting, invest in a bacteria/enzyme product.

Bacteria/Enzyme Digester

This is the most complete method of odor control, because it strikes the root of the problem and eliminates the very source of the bad odor. Bacteria/enzyme digesters actually feed on the organic compounds that are responsible for the bad odor of materials like urine, feces, vomit, mildew, etc. The most effective products contain a culture of friendly live bacteria, which lies dormant until you mix it with warm water.

When you put a bacteria/enzyme digester solution on an organic stain, the bacteria immediately start producing enzymes, which break down the organic compounds in the stain into substances the bacteria can use for food, just as the enzymes in our stomach break down the foods we eat into things we can digest. If they're kept moist and within the recommended temperature range (above 40° F), the bacteria will continue to eat the offending organic materials, reproduce, produce more enzymes, and eat some more until the odor-causing material is all gone.

You can get products composed of the enzymes alone, but they work only until the enzymes are used up, and require you to rinse away the remains of what the enzymes digested—how are you going to rinse underneath the carpet (where many pet stains penetrate), for example? The products that contain a live bacteria culture are better, or a bacteria culture plus some enzyme to get them started.

Bacteria/enzyme solutions are safe to use on any surface that can't be damaged by water, but they must be used by themselves, and can't be combined with detergents, deodorants, or other cleaning preparations. You should never use a disinfectant or any other chemical on the spot before applying the bacteria/enzyme solution because these things can actually kill the beneficial bacteria that destroy the odor.

You can't mix up the solution and save it for later, because the minute you add water the bacteria become active, and they die if you don't give them something to eat within ten hours. Nor is enzyme digestion an instant gratification process—when you treat something with a bacteria/enzyme product, it has to stay wet with the solution for six to eight hours. And since it contains no cleaning agent, you usually have to follow up a bacteria/enzyme digester with a pet stain remover or spotting chemical such as Nilotex, Dog-Tex, or Outright Foaming Pet Stain Eliminator, to remove surface stains or water rings.

But despite their drawbacks, enzymes are about the only way of eliminating entrenched odors in carpets, so they definitely have their place. They also work better than the chemical deodorizers on hard porous materials like concrete, because they penetrate the pores of the surface and eat away the organic materials that cause odor. Be sure to soak the area well with the solution and get it down to all the cracks and crevices where organic material may be lodged.

A bacteria/enzyme product I've found especially effective is Outright Pet Odor Eliminator, distributed by the Bramton Company of Dallas. Outright can be used on any water-safe surface or material including carpet, upholstery, drapes, mattresses, clothing, fabrics, tile, terrazzo, wood, metal, plastic, foam rubber, vinyl, concrete, trash containers, and even grass and shrubbery. Nontoxic, pleasant smelling, and all natural.

Since the bacteria/enzyme digesters are somewhat complicated to use, you'll probably want to save them for the more serious stain and odor situations, and use a chemical deodorizer/cleaner for less severe stains.

PLASTIC TRIGGER-SPRAY BOTTLE

These are handy for applying bacteria/enzyme or chemical deodorizer solution, as well as for misting plants, dampening laundry, and a score of other household uses. They also serve as a harmless, effective, and inexpensive pet training tool (see page 16). Professional-strength spray bottles are available in 16-, 22-, and 32-ounce sizes.

CARPET SPOT REMOVAL BRUSH

A stain should never be scrubbed, as this can damage the carpet fibers as well as spread the stain. This 10-inch wooden brush has short, stiff nylon bristles that enable you to pound on a spot with the brush to "agitate" the fibers without spreading the stain. The end of the handle is tapered to a sharp edge so you can use it to scrape up as much of the spot or spill as you can before applying the spotting or stain-removing chemical.

PROFESSIONAL CLEANING TOWEL

For all those jobs that require wiping and absorbing—and especially for stain removal—this is far better for the purpose than whatever happens to be resting in the rag bag. Made from a piece of sturdy terry toweling, it's sewn in a tube shape that gives you sixteen surfaces to clean with.

ABSORBENT COMPOUND

Sprinkle these highly absorbent clay granules on pet messes like vomit and loose stools and in no time flat the mess is solid enough to sweep, scoop, or vacuum up. Some compounds deodorize too, making the cleaning operation faster and more pleasant. (Big D Granular Deodorant, from Big D Industries, is a good brand.)

STAIN REPELLENT

not only helps to keep your carpet, furniture, upholstery, and fabric pet accessories cleaner in general, it also helps keep stains and spills from soaking in and possibly doing permanent damage. Good brands are Stain-Shield and Nilodor's Pet Proof.

AREA DEODORIZER

For room deodorizing, there are literally hundreds of products on the market, from aerosol sprays and stickup doodads to battery-powered dispensers. Spraying perfumed aerosol room deodorizers around will mask odors for a short while, but has little lasting effect. For the home, probably the best choice for ongoing deodorizing in a pet area is one of the stickup types or an oil-based deodorant in a small wick bottle, which can be tucked away in a hidden place and will work for a month or more. These products neutralize pet odors to an extent, and provide a pleasant masking fragrance. Personally, I prefer the scent of the natural oils in products like Nilodor and Big D wicks to the products with strong floral fragrances.

As with any odor problem, good ventilation is a real plus. Circulating air does a lot to keep an area fresh and free of animal odors, so in a heavy pet concentration area consider a vent to the outside with a fan that will draw the odor out and bring fresh air in. You especially want to get odor out before it can be absorbed by soft materials. A

POKE
POKE

room with lots of upholstery and carpeting will be smellier than a room with a tile floor and wood furniture, because there are more soft surfaces to absorb odor. This is a good reason to put odor-generating litter boxes, pet beds, etc. in a room with a hard floor and hard surface furnishings.

CARPET DEODORIZER

Carpet is a perfect "wick" to absorb odors, and most ordinary carpet shampoos remove dirt, but not odors. When you're trying to cope with this particular problem, beware of the ads that encourage you to "sprinkle a little Smellzgood carpet deodorizer on the spot where Fido lies, then just vacuum it up for a sweet-smelling dog and carpet." Some of these products can produce contact dermatitis on a dog's sensitive belly skin. If you want to sprinkle something on your carpet to make it smell better, baking soda does as good a job of deodorizing as anything and it won't bother your pet. (But it might clog your vacuum, and baking soda does absorb moisture and is a little abrasive to carpet fibers.) Nilo-fresh from the Nilodor Company is a corncob-based preparation that's safe to use around pets and is one of the few products that's actually been tested and

proven to work well and safely for this purpose.

If the situation is beyond a sprinkle-on solution, first vacuum the area with a good beater-bar vacuum. Then apply a bacteria/enzyme product according to label directions to loosen and digest pet skin oils, etc. When the bacteria solution has finished working, hand-shampoo the spot with carpet shampoo to which you've added a little water-soluble deodorant such as Nilodor Surface Deodorizer, or use Nilodor Deodorizing Carpet Shampoo. Just dip a nylon scrub brush in the solution and scrub briskly to work up a good lather. Then blot up the suds with a towel or a wet/dry vacuum. While the nap is still wet, brush it first one way and then the other with a dry stiff brush to get it all fluffed up. Brush the nap all in one direction to finish it off, and let it dry.

DEODORIZERS FOR USE ON YOUR PET HIMSELF

Regular bathing and grooming will do a lot to keep pet odor down. There are special shampoos formulated to help control pet body odor, too, such as Nilodor Deodorizing Shampoo and P.O.N. (Puppy Odor Neutralizer) shampoo.

A lot of pet body odor is hormonal, such as the pungent smell male cats have. Once you alter the animal a lot of the musky odor is gone. The same goes for a lot of other animals. Much pet body odor is sexual odor, an attraction odor. To reduce this, you have to spay or neuter the animal.

Then, too, much of the odor associated with our canine companions is the result of the secretions of the tiny oil glands an animal has all over its skin, especially inside the ears and around the genitals and other bare skin areas. For the basic everyday dog odor, there are products designed to spray directly on a dog's coat and skin to keep him smelling better between baths. Two I recommend are Robinson Labs' Dog Deodorant and Outright's Pet Odor Eliminator, a bacteria/enzyme deodorizer that can be used right on the pet itself. These will also work well on the rolled-in-something-awful odors a pet will often come home with.

But when skin odor is very pronounced and hard to control, your dog may be battling a case of dermatitis, which could be an allergic reaction to fleas, for example. Cases like this should be referred to your vet for treatment.

SKUNK ODOR REMOVER

When your dog has a close encounter of the worst kind, go to the pet store and get one of the new products designed specifically to counteract skunk odor. Most of these are of the enzyme or bacteria/enzyme digester variety, and can be used without even washing the dog first. A number of good products of this type are available, such as Skunk-Kleen from G. G. Bean, Inc. of Brunswick, ME, Skunk-Off, from the Thornell Corporation of Penfield, NY, Outright Skunk Odor Eliminator, and Odormute, from the Ryter Corporation. Most of these products will also work well on other pet body odors, and they

can also be used to remove skunk odor from household surfaces, rooms, clothes, etc.

When doing skunk cleanup, you need to really soak your pet with the solution, especially if it's a long-haired animal. And if your pet was hit by a skunk at close range it may be necessary to repeat the treatment.

A SUPERIOR SCOOPER

Well here it is, pet owners, the bottom line, the biggest single pet cleaning problem. It's the ultimate reality of animal ownership—the cleaning of the potty. We have quite a few choices here, at prices ranging from $4 to $30. The arsenal of available scooping hardware notwithstanding, the ordinary plastic bag is the hands-down favorite with experienced scoopers for pickup on the go. Basic bag technique is as follows: You carry a couple of bags in your purse or pocket, and when the moment of truth comes you pull out a bag and stick your hand in it, grab the pile, and pull the bag over your hand, turning it inside out as you go. Then knot the bag closed and drop it in the nearest receptacle.

You don't even have buy special bags. To quote *Dog Fancy:* "Perhaps the most practical, get-down-to-business device for scooping litter is the plastic bag that comes on the daily paper. Many dog walkers believe that this long plastic bag is the best follow-up for a messy dog because it doesn't cost a thing (unless you don't subscribe to a newspaper) and in fact disposes of an object that would otherwise clutter some kitchen corner." The bags such as those made to hold onions and other smelly foods in the refrigerator don't transfer odors, and people are getting hip to these.

You can buy black or otherwise opaque bags—there are even opaque bags that come complete with drawstrings or are shaped like mittens. And there are collapsible scooping frames for plastic bags such as the Doggie Bagg-Grr that are small enough to be carried discreetly while still providing a more remote means of pickup. If you go for bags alone, carry a paper lunch sack along with your plastic bag supply—so you've got a handy means of carrying *and* concealment along if it turns out to be a ways to the trash container.

Then there are the arm's-length scoopers, which are great for yard cleanup, but often take two hands to operate and are too cumbersome to carry on a walk. One staple is the long-handled dustpan with matching rake or shovel, which comes as two separate pieces, or connected in the middle. In metal scoopers, stainless steel is probably the most durable and cleanable, with chrome plated the next best.

The butterfly net scoopers are popular because they're lightweight and only take one hand to operate, which makes them more manageable for scooping on the go. They usually consist of a plastic bag suspended at the end of an aluminum frame. Some of the butterfly scoops collapse for ease of carrying, then unfold with a flick of the wrist into a full-length scooper. Some of these

also feature water-soluble bags that can be flushed down a toilet, or allow you to use ordinary Ziploc bags from the supermarket. Two of the best butterfly scoops are the Scoop-All and Scoop-a-Poo.

Scooping equipment should be cleaned and/or disinfected after every use. Use a nylon scrub brush and a good cleaner/deodorizer like Nilodor's Deodorizing Cleaner, or a Chlorasan solution (after first washing the equipment in detergent water and rinsing, to be sure the disinfectant has a chance to be fully effective).

Clean with Distraction Action

I'm a professional salesman of cleaning supplies, but I guarantee that a good quality toy can be a better investment than the best piece of cleaning equipment on the market. Good, strong, carefully chosen toys will entertain and exercise your pet for hours and help divert all that nervous energy. Like kids, tired animals *sleep!*

If you give cats, for example, their own "furniture" with a built-in gym, and all kinds of interesting nooks and hideouts and perches and platforms and textures, they'll spend less time somersaulting off the rockers and excavating your planters. And a stout scratching post is a must in every house with a cat. The Felix Katnip Tree is one of the best scratching posts available. It has a broad, sturdy base and a solid cedar post covered with tightly woven sisal fiber. Cats prefer a rough, tough surface like this to the carpeting found on many posts, and this post won't crumble or shed particles like cork or log posts do. It's even impregnated with catnip for extra cat appeal.

It would take a whole book to show all the kinds of toys and exercise equipment available for animals; pets love the toys you can make out of ordinary household objects and supplies, too. The bottom line is "what do they really like; what occupies them the most intensely and for the longest time?" (If they convert a pair of rubber thongs into quintuplets, maybe a sturdy rubber toy is the ticket.) When you figure out what they like, buy it or make it. Just remember that with toys, quality is important, safety is essential, and rotation is the key to long-term diversion and entertainment.

Shake, Rattle, and Rig! (More Important Tools for the Pet Cleaner)

These devices give that old famous "negative feedback" on the act you're trying to discourage. Your cat or dog does something wrong and you correct him with one of these, and he comes to realize that something he really dislikes happens when he does a certain thing, so he stops doing that thing. It may take five tries, it may take fifty, but after a while he'll get the idea.

Squirt Bottle

Thousands of experienced pet owners and trainers agree—this is one of the gentlest and most effective disciplinary measures around. When you catch your pet in the act of misbehaving (chewing furniture, jumping on the table, making long-distance phone calls), simply squirt him with plain water. The quickness of your draw is important in this particular type of pet correction—not more than *two seconds* should go by between the forbidden act and your discouraging squirt.

The Scat bottle (that's what I call it) is the same type of professional spray bottle used in the cleaning industry. It holds an entire quart and can send a steady stream of water at least twenty feet. If your cat decides to snack on one of your houseplants, give him a squirt from across the room. This is a useful behavior modification tool for dogs, too. If you have a large dog or one with thick fur, you might have to squirt him in the face to get his attention. A little fresh lemon juice added to the water may also make a spray bottle a more effective discourager of dogs. Put a few spray bottles in different rooms for when you need them. If the quart size is a little too hefty for you to handle, professional-strength spray bottles are available in 22-, and even 16-ounce sizes.

The main drawback of a squirt bottle is that it only works when you're home to use it. And you never want to misuse or overuse the spray bottle technique. Spraying your pet without good reason could bring on behavior problems or cause him to fear and avoid you. And always use only *plain water*—or the water/lemon juice solution.

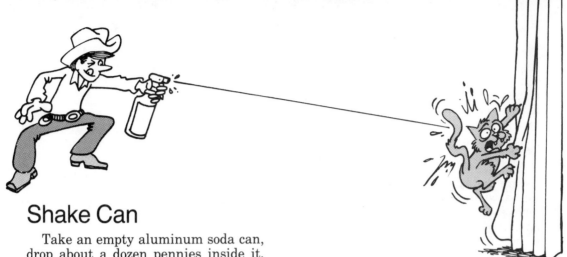

Shake Can

Take an empty aluminum soda can, drop about a dozen pennies inside it, cover the hole with a piece of strong tape, and you've got yourself a tool for commanding your pet's attention—close up or from a distance.

When you see your pet doing something he shouldn't, say "No," and give the can a good shake. The surprisingly loud and obnoxious rattle that results is usually enough to convince your pet to cease and desist. Make a few shake cans and put them in different places in the house so no matter where you are you can shake your pet into remembering his manners.

You can also toss a shake can near where the pet is misbehaving, being careful not to hit him. After a while, you may even be able to just set a shake can on objects your pet isn't supposed to get on or near, and he'll stay away.

Throw Chain

A throw chain is just a short length of chain, usually a dog slip collar, used the same way as a thrown shake can—throw it near a pet and it makes a loud, startling noise. You can just put a slip chain in your pocket till you need it. (Again, be sure you don't hit the animal with the chain, just toss it so it'll land near him.)

Booby Traps

A booby trap is designed to discourage a pet from a particular behavior, even if you're *not* there to catch him at it. You can put some good old Yankee ingenuity to work here to think of additional ways to put your pet off without ever hurting or seriously frightening him.

If at all possible, use booby traps when you're home and can keep an eye on your pet. If he happens to get really frightened by a booby trap going off, worse things than what you're trying to discourage him from might happen.

SHAKE CAN TRAPS

If your cat is jumping on the counters when you're not home, or the dog is stealing goodies out of the garbage cans, or swiping laundry from the basket, you can set up shake cans as a booby trap.

For example, in the case of pets getting into the garbage, set a piece of cardboard on top of several shake cans on a shelf, counter, or table above the garbage can. Then balance more cans in a pyramid shape on top of the cardboard. Tie a piece of string from one of the bottom cans to a piece of paper towel that has a bit of bacon grease on it and put the baited towel in the garbage can. Don't use an actual goody like a sandwich for bait because you don't want to reward the dog in case he manages to steal it.

When the dog reaches in for the bait and starts to take it out, the string will pull the bottom can out from under the cardboard and the cans will crash down. Even if you have a Doberman who eats hubcaps for breakfast, after this happens a couple of times, he wouldn't reach into the garbage even if you left a sirloin steak in there.

Empty cardboard boxes can serve as well as shake cans for a harmless avalanche effect. And shake cans can also be hung from the curtain rod with strings to protect imperiled drapes.

MOUSETRAPS

If your dog or cat jumps up on something you don't want him to when you're not home or in sight, take a few mousetraps, set them, and turn them upside down on the object you're trying to protect. Place a sheet of newspaper lightly on top of them, and tape or weight the paper down to keep it from slipping off or a pet's paw from getting trapped. When the pet climbs up on the "loaded" surface, the traps will give a loud *snap* and startle him into jumping off. After this happens a few times, the pet's going to think, "Boy, I hate it when that couch snaps at me. I think I'll go lie down in my bed instead."

BALLOONS

are another noisy surprise that pets don't appreciate. They're most useful as a deterrent for medium to large dogs because dogs are heavier than cats and their claws are always out. Tape the balloons to the seat cushion of the sofa or chair, for example, and when the dog jumps up and steps on a balloon, the loud pop will get him skedaddling off fast. Or attach balloons to the window, door, curtain, etc., your pet has been clawing.

If you want to be *sure* balloons turn your pet off, pop a couple of them right near him. It's very likely then that just taping a balloon or two to something will render it repulsive.

NETTING

can serve as a cat deterrent. If your cat, for example, continues to scratch away at your furniture even after you've gotten him a scratching post, try using netting (the kind you get to keep the cardinals off the cherry tree) and spread it over the area that's being scratched or climbed. Cats don't like to snag their claws, so they may decide they like the scratching post better after all.

PLASTIC WRAP AND FOIL

is another way to discourage cats, especially, from areas you don't want them in or on. Cover or protect the thing in question with plastic sheeting, plastic wrap, or aluminum foil—most cats and dogs don't like walking or lying on these.

Before using any of these techniques, give some thought to which fit best with your pet's personality. A shy or nervous animal and a highly aggressive one call for different approaches.

Cats are somewhat harder to train using these devices than dogs. A dog will soon get to the point where he won't chew the sofa pillow even when you're gone because he had such a horrible experience with it when you were home. But cats seem to be able to put things together: "If she's here and this is here, I can't do it, but if she's *not* here and this is here I can do it." It's not that cats are necessarily smarter than dogs, but somehow they often understand that the catastrophe only happens when another element is present, and the other element is you.

Whatever technique you use, it's important to always show your pet afterward what they *are* permitted to chew or lie down or scratch on. And when they go and do what you want them to do instead, be sure to praise them.

CHAPTER 2

Good Clean Living— with Pets

Dear Don,

I want to confess a couple of concerns I have about pet cleanup. I don't think I'm an antigerm fanatic, but animals do seem rather dirty, and the thought of my baby crawling across the floor (where the dog may have walked, rolled, or even dragged his behind) simply makes my hair stand on end.

I never let the dog up on the bed or furniture, and after little Joey's wrapped his crib blanket around our pup, do I need to throw it right in the washer? (For that matter, is it okay to wash pet bedding in the very same machine used for people clothes?) Am I right to get uptight every time I catch the kids sharing their snacks with the cat, or playing with our pets' toys, or letting the dog lick their hands or faces?

And just how germy is the dog bowl? I never want to wash it in the kitchen sink where people food is made; I clean and rinse it outside and throw the dirty water over the fence or down the toilet. Am I being over-cautious?

Sincerely,

Annie Septic

Annie Septic

We've all known people who get over-excited about real or imagined ailments in themselves or others, especially if the disease is unusual or exotic—or from an exotic source, such as pets. As one of this country's top physicians said on a national program I appeared on not long ago, "In the average general family practice, over two-thirds of the patients that come groaning and sniffling in for office visits don't need to. They have something that time, rest, or a good bar of soap will eventually cure by itself." Worries about pet diseases can be the same. Though most diseases and parasites are quite particular and usually stick to a single species, there are some diseases that animals can transmit to us. All in all, about sixty-five different kinds, though less than thirty are reasonably common.

The chances of you catching a disease from your pet—especially if you've had him vaccinated against all the things your vet recommends—are actually quite remote. Yes, a dog's skin and tongue are literally crawling with bacteria—but then so are ours. Most of these "bugs" are friendly and even useful, and the chances of catching something unpleasant from an animal are far less than the chance of catching it from another person. The odds are definitely in your favor, especially if you follow the basic rules of sanitation, or simple cleanliness, described in the following pages.

The Floor

The floor is the final catchall—for fallout from the sky, air, people, and pets. And floors in a pet home should be kept extra clean. Especially if you have crawling children, for example, who put everything in their mouths. For the three to six months that your child crawls, I'd do "double duty" on the floor.

Keep a spray bottle of disinfectant solution near the damp mop and then every other day quickly spray the floor with it. Let it sit on there for ten minutes and then run the mop over it, and rinse well. This will pick up the dirt and kill any potential disease-causing germs.

When cleaning hard floors in pet areas, use a little bit of water-soluble odor neutralizer such as Nilodor's Surface Deodorizer in your cleaning solution, or use a one-step cleaner and deodorizer such as Nilodor Deodorizing Cleaner from time to time, to keep things smelling sweet.

Walls

The walls in the average home are washed about once a year, though this varies with the lifestyle of the inhabitants (smokers and people with wood-stoves do have to wash walls more often.) With pets, as with kids, you'll probably be spot-cleaning more often. You also don't want to let grease build up and stay on walls, because that sticky film will hold hair, dust, dander, and germs. So an overall wall-washing every six months or so in areas like the kitchen might be called for.

If you have a pet who sprays, you'll want to wash the lower parts of walls (up to at least eighteen inches) and the baseboards, etc., more frequently, and add a water-soluble deodorant such as Nilodor Surface Deodorizer to your cleaning solution. This is a good idea in any room where pet odor might be a problem.

Particular areas of the wall that get a lot of pet body contact—such as the spots where a pet leans against the wall when he beds down—should be disinfected (washed or sprayed with Chlorasan solution that's left on at least ten minutes, and then rinsed well) from time to time.

Easy Ways to Control Pet Diseases

Most diseases are spread by coming in direct contact with pet excretions or secretions (or infected surfaces or materials) and then failing to wash your hands. You don't need to be a chemist or professional cleaner to prevent the spread of disease—just be consistent. Simple cleanliness is the best defense.

Always wash your hands after playing with a pet and after cleaning the litter box or cleaning up pet accidents, or doing scooping duty, or cleaning a cage.

Don't touch your mouth, nose, or eyes, and don't eat or prepare food while handling an animal. Also control "extra-close contact" with pets. Yes, this means things like kissing pets and letting them sleep in your bed or lie on your pillow and letting them lick people's hands and faces. Young children, especially, can catch pet diseases this way, so set clear-cut rules for kids with pets.

Keep pet potty areas cleaned up promptly. Pick up and dispose of pet fe-ces at least daily. Many pet diseases are spread by contact with the wastes of an infected animal, so if you keep things clean you'll avoid problems.

Dispose of soiled cat litter promptly, in a sealed bag or container, and keep the litter box away from areas where food is prepared. Outdoors, don't let your cat use the kids' sandbox as a litter box—keep it covered when not in use, because parasites and diseases can be passed on all too easily this way.

Rain dissolves and distributes animal wastes, or they dry to dust, so they're often no longer visible, but if a child plays in the area he can be infected when he puts his fingers, toys, etc., in his mouth. Don't let the children's play area be one that's regularly littered with dog stools—and you especially don't want children to run barefoot or play scantily clothed in such areas.

Roundworm eggs or hookworm larvae, for example, can often be found in dog feces, and they can live a long time in the dirt. Worms that infest pets can't usually survive to fulfill their whole life cycle in the human body, but they can invade humans occasionally and do some damage (to children especially) before they succumb.

Keeping your pet free of fleas will reduce the chances of infection, too. Children can swallow an infected flea and get tapeworm, and a number of other diseases (including the bubonic plague) are spread by fleas. See page 88 for flea control measures for your pet and his whole environment.

Rocky Mountain spotted fever is spread by ticks and is found in areas of the country other than the Rockies now. Apply tick remedies when they seem called for to keep ticks off your pet. Be careful when removing ticks; use a tissue moistened with rubbing alcohol or straight household ammonia and avoid touching the tick itself.

Keeping the family pets free of worms is one of the most important ways of preventing the spread of disease. Be sure a puppy or kitten has been dewormed before you get him, and have your pet checked regularly for worms. Bring a stool sample with you each time you go to the vet—the test only takes ten minutes! If your pet spends time in areas littered with the feces of other pets or does hunt and eat small animals, have him checked at least twice a year. Let the vet prescribe medication if it's needed. Do-it-yourself wormers are dangerous as well as often not fully effective.

Toxoplasmosis is a tiny single-celled parasite that cats can carry. The disease isn't common, but since the intermediate host for the disease is mice, cats that hunt are more likely to get it. If a cat has this parasite, and the litter box isn't cleaned of feces at least every two days, the spores from the parasite, which are transmitted by air, will develop to the infective stage.

The disease is most dangerous to pregnant women because the parasite settles inside the unborn child, and can result in serious birth defects such as mental retardation. If you're pregnant, you should either have someone else clean out the litter box or, if you do it, make sure you do so every day. Or use disposable boxes. A free pamphlet about toxoplasmosis is available from the Iams Company. Write: NIAID Booklet, The Iams Company, P.O. Box 826, Lewisburg, OH 45338.

Prevention Is the Best Medicine

Avoid problems to begin with by keeping your pet healthy.

- *Feed him a nutritious, balanced diet, and clean his food and water bowls regularly.*

- *Keep him clean by regular grooming.*

- *Make sure he has a checkup at least once a year, and all the vaccinations your vet recommends.*

- *Don't let your pet hunt and eat mice, rabbits, squirrels, etc., or even earthworms. All of these can carry parasites and diseases to your pet, and then possibly to you.*

- *Don't let your pet run loose. This is one sure way of picking up diseases from other animals. A fenced yard will keep your dog in and other dogs out.*

- *Keep any cage, run, or enclosure your pet spends time in clean and free of accumulated droppings.*

- *Make sure your pet's sleeping quarters are clean, dry, and warm (to prevent the chills and drafts that bring on diseases). Remove soiled bedding promptly.*

- *Clean your pet's toys and accessories, too, from time to time.*

- *Beware of exotic pets: Among the many good reasons not to keep a wild* animal as a pet is the fact that a number of diseases can be spread to humans by contact with wild animals, or by wild animals that come in contact with our pets.

- *Clean, and apply antiseptic to, scratches and superficial cuts on your pet as soon as they appear so infection won't have a chance to penetrate or be spread this way. And if a pet has sores or other skin lesions, keep your—and your children's—hands away from them. Don't handle an animal if you have an open wound.*

Precautions for Ill Pets

Isolate a sick pet from the other pets in the house. Confine him to a single out-of-the-way area or a quiet room, preferably one with a seamless or well-sealed hard floor and nonabsorbent walls and furniture.

Exchange his regular bedding for disposable bedding such as a cardboard box filled with shredded newspaper. Don't shake a sick pet's blanket in the house, and remember to dispose of soiled bedding promptly. Minimize your handling of him as much as you can, and wash your hands well after touching him or his food dishes, bedding, wound dressings, etc.

You especially don't want to allow children to handle a sick animal— young children and the elderly are always more susceptible to infection. And no one who has an immunosuppressive disease, is on chemotherapy, or has had an organ transplant should handle a sick animal, because in all of these cases the person involved has a weakened immune system. It's not that they'll necessarily catch what the animal has, but sick animals can easily come down with secondary infections such as strep and staph and we *can* get those diseases.

A Word of Caution about Disinfectants

It was one of my first professional cleaning jobs and like most novices in cleaning, I was sure the stronger a solution was, the better it must work! That straight commercial ammonia I was using in the stuffy little sewing room was hard to take and I stumbled out occasionally for a breath of fresh air. When I was finished, the woman of the house came running out screaming, "My bird is dead, my bird is dead!" And it was.

It's a terrible feeling to know you've harmed a helpless animal because of carelessness, and believe it or not, it's common. In our efforts to clean and care for our pets, we often unknowingly harm them.

The idea of "disinfecting" seizes us almost like a crusade or holy war. We'll apply a disinfectant, by gosh, and really zap any little undesirables that might be invading our premises. But even doctors and vets will testify that good, thorough *cleaning* of pet areas and articles will go a long way toward keeping pets and people healthy and free of disease. As one head of Hospital Infection Control put it, "elbow grease is one of the best disinfectants." How well and regularly you clean is more important than precisely what you use, even when it comes to keeping germs at bay.

When and What to Disinfect

What pet areas and objects should you keep good and clean all the time, and disinfect from time to time, especially if you have a number of pets or pets that spend a fair amount of time outdoors?

- *Pet food and water dishes*

- *The floor and walls near the pet feeding area*

- *Your pet's bed*

- *The concrete or gravel surfaces of dog runs and kennels and backyard "pet potty" areas*

- *Gutters and drains in dog runs and kennels*

- *Litter pans and spoons, and the walls and floor around the litter box*

- *The toilet bowl if the cat uses it, and the tub or shower if the litter box is kept there*

- *Scooping equipment*

- *Waste containers used for pet purposes, such as dumping used litter*

- *Pet cages and crates*

- *Furniture surfaces or walls or drapes that a pet spends a lot of time lounging against*

- *Your pet's food bowls, cage or crate, toys, etc., after he's been sick or kept at a boarding kennel (not a few pet diseases are picked up this way)*

- *The bed, general area, and accessories that a pet who had a serious infectious disease used or inhabited, before you bring home a new pet*

- *The doghouse*

WHAT ABOUT BLEACH AS A DISINFECTANT?

Many vets and kennels use a bleach solution as a general disinfectant—mainly because it's the only thing that's 100 percent effective against the viruses that cause the serious diseases of parvovirus in dogs and panleukopenia in cats. But bleach has a strong odor, can damage many household surfaces, and its disinfecting action is seriously impaired by "organic matter" (urine, feces, dirt, grass, pet hair, etc.). And with all the different cleaners we use in the home today, there's always a danger of someone unknowingly mixing another chemical with bleach, resulting in dan-

gerous or even lethal chemical reactions. So, unless your vet specifically recommends bleach for a particular home cleaning situation, there are better things for the job.

OTHER COMMON DISINFECTANTS

Among the most commonly used disinfectants not long ago were the phenolics (made from phenol, or carbolic acid). Phenolics, especially in low concentrations, are generally safe for humans to use and store—many household disinfectants are phenol derivatives but they can be lethal to cats and some other animals. Phenolic disinfectants are not recommended for use around pets by most experts. Some products, such as Lysol Spray Disinfectant, contain orthophenylphenol, a synthetic derivative of phenol, that's considered far less toxic to animals than phenol itself. But I hesitate to recommend the use of any phenol-based disinfectant around small animals, because the potential for harm is certainly there.

The quaternary disinfectants, or "quats," which have an ammonium chloride base, are safer to use around pets than phenolics, and most of them have a general-purpose cleaner added, so the solution cleans as it disinfects. These are widely used today, but many manufacturers won't package quaternary disinfectants for home use because of the potential dangers to people. Quats are skin and eye irritants, and their fumes or mist can damage mucous membranes. They are seriously toxic if ingested. I hesitate to recommend the use of a product of this nature in the home.

This doesn't mean you should rush to the pine-oil products for the purpose, even if they do smell nice and natural.

That piney fragrance is their strongest point—they're neither particularly good cleaners nor disinfectants, and they, too, can be dangerous to pets. (If a pine-oil product solution gets on a pet's footpads, for example, it's ingested when the pet licks its paws.)

THE SAFEST DISINFECTANT

For situations that do call for a true disinfectant, Chlorasan, manufactured by Franklin Labs of Fort Dodge, Iowa, is the one I'd use. It does a better job of destroying viruses, fungi, and bacteria than quaternary or phenolic disinfectants, yet is far less likely to sting, burn, or cause skin irritation or reaction than any other disinfectant available. (It's gentle enough that it can be, and is, used in ointments and surgical wound cleansers.) It's much less dangerous if a pet *did* happen to accidently ingest a small amount of the solution, and it can even be safely used to disinfect birdcages and small animal cages. It's usually available only through vets and pet stores, and is used extensively for disinfecting animal hospitals, farm premises, dog kennels, and pet equipment. But Franklin Labs agreed to make it available directly to the consumer by mail for the first time. (See page 5 for the address of Housework, Inc.)

When using Chlorasan for general disinfecting purposes, dilute it one ounce to a gallon of water before using. For disinfection of areas known to be harboring diseases, the ratio is usually upped to three ounces to a gallon of water. Chlorasan will even kill at least 96 percent of any parvovirus organisms present if you apply it in a stronger than usual concentration (16 ounces to a gallon of water) and leave it on for a longer time than usual (an hour or so) before rinsing.

25

Some General Rules for Using Disinfectants

1. *Whenever you're performing a major cleaning operation, keep the pets away until you're finished. Never use a disinfectant on the animal itself, and remove food and water dishes, toys, etc. from the area before you apply a disinfectant.*

2. *Be sure to clean the area or object well first. A solution has to get to the surface of something to be able to disinfect it, and if that surface is covered with dirt and litter it can't. Besides, the germ-killing powers of most disinfectants are seriously weakened by the presence of "organic matter"—things like hair, excrement, dirt, dander, uneaten food, milk, and many types of bedding materials. So scrape and brush and sweep first, but not so vigorously that you stir up a cloud of dust— that's an excellent way to spread disease germs through the air. It's also important to rinse well after the precleaning.*

3. *Don't mix a disinfectant with other cleaning products unless the label tells you it's okay to do so—and then, only use the kind specified. Follow the dilution and other directions on the label to the letter—never make the solution stronger than it says.*

4. *Use disinfectants with care, as many are irritating to the skin and can be absorbed through it. (You may want to wear rubber gloves.) Avoid spilling or splashing the solution on yourself or in your eyes. Likewise, don't mist a disinfectant solution or apply it in a very fine spray; when chemicals are sprayed in a fine mist they can be inhaled easily and may* be dangerous to the lungs and bodies of pets and people alike. Avoid aerosols whenever you can, for your own sake as well as your pet's. The mist from an aerosol can is finer and stays airborne longer. (If you must spray, squirt a small amount onto your cleaning cloth, rather than filling the air with spray.)

5. *When applying disinfectant, really saturate the surface with the solution. Don't forget the crevices, cracks, and corners. Where would you hide, if you were a germ?*

6. *Leave the solution on the surface for at least ten minutes.*

7. *Then rinse well with clean water to remove the chemicals.*

8. *To disinfect fabric items, soak them in a bucket or tub of disinfectant solution for at least fifteen minutes, before putting them through the usual washing process. Disinfectant can also be added to the final rinse cycle, instead.*

9. *Air out or dry the disinfected articles or areas well before putting them back in use.*

10. *Store disinfectants in a secure place (preferably a locked place, well out of the reach of children and pets) and don't buy them in too large a quantity at one time.*

Sane Storage of Pet Supplies

Pet feeding and care is done daily, so why not set up a special storage area for the pet food and supplies, a handy place that's easy to use and clean and keeps the critters from getting into it?

Pet Control Center

1. hooks for leashes, slip chains, etc.
2. scooper, dustpan, broom
3. dispensers for large and small plastic bags
4. suspended food hopper/dispenser
5. suspended food and water dishes
6. pet placemat to catch spills
7. visible storage of grooming tools, with sharp tools stored high
8. pet grooming platform
9. built-in vacuum with pet grooming head
10. squeegee
11. large pull-out garbage can or storage bin
12. vent
13. heat lamp
14. extra food storage in plastic containers
15. spray bottles
16. paper towels
17. terry towels
18. shallow storage for pet medicine, vitamins, oils, etc.
19. shampoos and conditioners
20. removable spray head
21. low wash basin with six-inch lip to hold water in, set up on a 2½-foot cabinet so that you only have to bend slightly to use it. A good place to clean pet dishes and mats, dump dirty mop water, and wash off dirty pets
22. miscellaneous storage drawers
23. flea killers and disinfectants stored up high behind closed doors
24. pet cleaning cloths
25. rolled-up mats
26. one file-cabinet size drawer for pet records
27. suspended hopper to store and dispense cat litter
28. enclosed pull-out litter box

For the avid pet owner, a pet control center that really provides for every pet activity and cleaning project will concentrate and reduce the cleaning. It'll also solve some tough questions of storage, sanitation, and safety. A control center could take as little room as a big closet; near an outside door is a good place for it.

When you're planning your control center, bear in mind that shallow storage in which everything is immediately visible is by far the best. If everything is neat and clean and easy to get to, it's more likely to stay that way. You also want to be sure to store sharp or dangerous or potentially poisonous pet care items up where kids and pets can't get to them. Get them up high and even behind a locked door if necessary.

For dry food storage, don't trust the bag it comes in. Set the bag down inside of, or empty it into, a large clean plastic or metal can with a tight-fitting lid. Food stored in open containers or in plastic, paper, cloth or burlap bags is almost certain to become infested. For a strong pest-proof storage container, use a hard plastic or rubber garbage can, or the large metal containers that popcorn and potato chips are sometimes sold in. You can even use the big plastic containers with lids that fast-food stores will often sell you very inexpensively. Pet treats, etc., that come in cardboard boxes can be stored in sealable plastic containers after the box is opened. Plastic containers are really the best for all kinds of food—no dents, no rust, no noise.

Storing dry or semimoist pet food in a sturdy plastic or metal can eliminates pet food odors, keeps pests and pets from getting in, and keeps the sack from getting wet or breaking open. Cans like these come in handy, too, if you have enough pets to buy pet food or litter in bulk from a wholesale distributor, feed store, or farmers' co-op. You don't want to store anything directly on the floor, even in closed containers—it'll be susceptible to moisture and pests. Put your containers on sturdy open shelves at least eighteen inches off the floor.

Keep a deep metal cup or plastic container inside the can or hanging on a handy hook nearby for scooping; a tall narrow cup can be filled two-thirds full without letting anything spill out.

Don't get more dry food than your pet can use up in about a month—if these foods are stored too long they lose nutritional value through oxidation, etc. This is why you don't want to store pet foods in a hot place; in temperatures higher than normal room temperature they'll deteriorate quickly. And a damp place will encourage the growth of mold and mildew, as well as posing a rust risk to metal containers.

Clean the containers out every six months and wipe them down with a Chlorasan and water solution. Be sure to rinse and dry well before refilling.

Suspend Everything You Can

A sturdy plastic storage and dispensing bin that mounts on the wall will keep pet supplies clean, dry, convenient, and safe from pets and pests. I think it's the ideal way to store and handle dry pet food, birdseed, cat litter, and other dry materials such as soap powder or charcoal. The Handy Hopper brand even has a peephole to let you know when the supply is getting low, and a safety catch to keep it from dispensing accidentally.

If I were going to set up the ideal pet feeding situation, and didn't want to build an entire control center, I'd suspend the food storage right in the area where the pets are fed. A large plastic dispenser such as the Handy Hopper will let the food fall out right into the bowl. This would prevent mess from pouring or dropping food, and I wouldn't have to dip my hands into dry dog food twice a day. I'd set it about chest high so the animals couldn't get to it and I didn't have to bend over or stretch up to reach it.

Maintaining the Feeding Zone

Where do we usually locate the pet dining zone? Right in the heaviest traffic lane where everyone walks over or through—not only disturbing the pet at his meal but tracking stuff around and distributing it. Would you like to be served dinner in the middle of the busiest sidewalk in town? How do you suppose an animal feels being fed in hallways, by doorways, and on porches (we feed them there because it's handy to quickly dump the food in the dish and be done with it). We fed our cats and dogs by the side of the back door for so many years I began to spell dog with

AAAAAAAAH!!

MAX

two o's. It was always a mess.

Put the pet dining in a niche or private area where adults, children, and for that matter, other pets aren't constantly marching through. Find a place out of the traffic flow and out of drafts. Feed your pets in an area with hard-surface flooring, and choose one feeding place and stick with it. Pets appreciate the consistency of "same time, same place," and you don't need two or three feedlots to keep clean instead of one. If you have both cats and dogs, however, you might want to feed them at separate times or in different rooms.

If you crate your dog (see page 40), feeding him in the crate will cut down on feeding mess. And if you allow your dog a bone (an uncooked beef knuckle or soup bone only, for safety's sake), establish the crate as the only place bones are allowed. In any case, make sure your dog does his bone or treat chewing in one spot—don't let him drag these things all over.

Never feed on carpet or on porous surfaces like unsealed concrete or brick. Where there's food, THERE WILL ALWAYS BE SPILLAGE, by you and by the pet. Even the most Emily Post pet will slurp, splash, spill, dribble, and spread his food and water all over the area while eating.

PICK A GOOD PET DISH

Think of cleaning time and mess potential when you pick a pet dish. Individual dishes for individual pets is a wise and logical move—no pet likes another pet in competition for his food, and it'll save cleaning up "jealousy messes." Cats can share a water bowl with other cats, but not a food bowl.

You want round dishes so there are no corners that an animal can't lick clean, and the heavier and more unbreakable, the better. (This means no plastic margarine containers or lids!)

Some dishes have tip-proof designs, or weighted bottoms, so they can't be knocked over, slid along the floor, or carried off by an animal. A pet dish should also be tooth-proof; plastic and aluminum, for example, can be chewed. Pets can get dermatitis (sores around the mouth) from some plastic dishes; orange and yellow bowls seem to be the most common culprits. Plastic can also absorb odors and scientists even claim it very gradually dissolves over time, so avoid plastic dishes if possible.

Also avoid two-compartment feeders which, like two-compartment buckets, can put you into a rubber room! Both sides never need filling at once, and you can't effectively empty one side at a time—the food and water will slop or leak into each other. Get a separate dish for water and put it some distance from the food bowl, so your pets can't drop mouthfuls of half-eaten food into the water dish.

If you have a long-eared dog like a cocker spaniel, you want a narrow steep-sided bowl to keep your pet's ears from becoming messed and matted with food. Likewise, you want a deep dish for a long-nosed pet and a shallow one for pups, cats, and short-nosed dogs.

There are elevated food dishes for tall pets, too, but be sure such dishes are set in a sturdy stand, or the ease with which they can be knocked over will offset how much easier your pet can reach his food.

There are also dishes set in frames that can be attached to the wall, or to the side of the cage. A suspended bowl is much easier to clean up under, and it won't get knocked over. You can also install it at a height that's easier on the dog (he won't have to bend down so far to eat) and easier on you, because you won't have to bend down so far to serve.

Look for a suspended dish with a small ledge around it to catch the dribbles, and also consider putting a

splashboard of plastic laminate or vinyl on the wall in back of the dish. Stainless steel is almost indestructible and easy to clean in hot sterilizing water; it will never rust or rot. (In very cold climates you wouldn't want to use it outdoors, however.) Heavyweight ceramic or pottery dishes are next best.

BE PREPARED FOR SPILLS

Place a 2x3-foot nylon or plastic rubber-backed mat under the dishes. Then you can just pick up the mat from time to time and rinse it off or hose it down. The nonslip back will keep the mat in place and discourage your pet from dragging it around to play with it. You could also use a rubber bath mat (the kind with little suction feet), or a big shallow tray such as a low-sided plastic litter box or a cookie sheet. This will eliminate that dusty, grimy, crumby, sticky spot on the floor where the pet dishes are. All the mess and spillage is contained and after dinner you can simply take the tray to the sink for a quick cleanup. The floor and eating area will stay clean and sanitary.

Make sure whatever you use under the pet dishes is protective first, then absorbent. When something is totally absorbent, it generally also wets whatever's under it, so you end up cleaning any spills up off both things. (An old towel under there isn't too bad, but newspapers will just multiply the mess.)

SELF-FEEDERS

(for dry pet food, usually) sound like the best of all possible worlds, and in a few circumstances they can work well for pets, but they do have some disadvantages. The continuous presence of food in an open (or openable) container attracts pests and insects. Pets that continually eat and drink eliminate continually, too. And some pets *will* gobble their way to overweight in a self-feeding situation. Self-feeding is an especially bad idea for an unhousebroken dog.

The automatic waterers, on the other hand, can be a good idea if they're rust-proof and designed in such a way that the water can't become stale or freeze. But there are also problems with using an automatic waterer. Too often, people will just forget about a jug-type waterer until they notice it's empty, which could be long after it runs dry. It doesn't take long for water to become stagnant and for bacteria and algae to begin to accumulate; your pet's saliva will also collect on the bottom of the bowl. All of which will make the water taste bad and create a breeding place for germs. The automatic waterers that are constantly refilled with fresh water are better (and may be a good idea for a dog run or the like), but they still have the problem of saliva accumulation in the bowl. And I certainly wouldn't risk having one inside the house—if it got tipped over or somehow stuck open, you'd be left with soaked carpets, flooded rooms, and other expensive damage.

Outdoors, the type (such as the Lixit) that you attach to an outside faucet or garden hose so your pet can serve himself present the fewest cleaning and sanitation problems.

KEEP THE WATER CLEAN

It's important to be sure your pet always has fresh water on hand. This doesn't mean leave the water bowl on the floor and top it off from time to time with a little fresh water from the sink. At least once a day take up the water bowl, wash it out (with soap, not just water!), rinse it, and refill it with fresh, clean water. A constant supply of fresh water is essential for any cat or dog—and only more so

for those fed dry food, older pets, and pets kept outside, especially in summer. Cats, especially, are reluctant to drink stale or soiled water. If you do use a bowl-type automatic waterer, it's a good idea to disinfect it from time to time, especially if it's had an algae, etc., accumulation.

DON'T DODGE THE DISHES

Contrary to popular belief, pets' licking and the rain won't keep animal dishes clean, any more than us wiping our own dishes out with a crust or napkin will. Even if a pet dish is licked clean, it still has a sticky coating of saliva. Dirty animal dishes entice unwanted crawly intruders and breed bacteria and possible illness for animals and humans alike.

Wash pet food and water dishes at least every day. And don't be afraid to use the kitchen sink. Animal dishes generally aren't as dirty as ours. Just wash them in good hot dish detergent solution and rinse them like any others.

If you don't want to bowserize your immaculate sink with pet dishes, you can wash them in the utility sink, or in a plastic bucket.

To disinfect pet dishes, soak them in a Chlorasan solution for five or ten minutes after you've washed and rinsed them, and then rinse them well again before you put them back in service.

Feed the Right Food

What you feed your pet depends on its age and condition, and whether it's a cat or dog, but beyond the strict questions of nutrition, which your vet or a good book on the subject can advise you on, there are some KP concerns here, too. Obviously, the softer the food, the messier, because it splashes and drips and runs. Hard food, even if it's spilled, can be easily cleaned up by the pet or by us. And the experts agree that for most purely

You'd think someone could change my water once in a while.

"pet" cats and dogs, dry foods are fine. They're cheaper, less messy, and keep a pet's teeth cleaner. They can also be stored without refrigeration. Canned pet foods, or a mixture of canned and dry, may be necessary for older or very finicky animals, but otherwise, try to stick to dry. Canned foods are more expensive, messier to handle and clean up after, awkward to store, and tend to have strong odors. Moist foods are somewhere in between dry and canned—they have some of the advantages of each, but many experts think they contain too much sugar to be good for a pet's health.

CONSIDER A SPECIALTY FOOD

Among the 15,000 or more types of commercial dog and cat foods today are many kinds of specialty foods, such as those for pups, older animals, the "couch potato" or the extra-active pet.

A specialty food of particular interest to the pet cleaner are the "nutritionally dense" dog and cat foods. These cost more, but are carefully designed to provide 100 percent nutrition in a lesser amount of food. This means less to store, less to spoon out, and less to clean up. A pet eating such food also has smaller and fewer stools, and the stools are firmer and easier to deal with. They'll also be less foul-smelling than the droppings of dogs and cats fed the chock-full-of-cereal-filler "supermarket" pet foods.

Whatever food you do choose, try to stick with it. Frequent changes in diet produce digestive upsets, which means (messy!) diarrhea or vomiting.

For your sake—and for your pet's sake—don't allow him to eat from your table or around the table. Get him in the habit of eating in a certain place at a certain time. If you must feed him table scraps, make sure they're no more than 20 percent of his diet, and mix them with his regular food.

DON'T FEED TOO OFTEN, OR TOO MUCH

The experts agree that adult cats and dogs should be fed only a couple of times a day, and they can get by with just once. (The wild relatives of our pets can go for several days eating only once and staying strong and healthy.) If pets munch and lap all day off and on, their whole life becomes eating and voiding, and yours feeding and cleaning! Nor is it good for a pet's health, over time, to have his system constantly focused on eating and digesting.

It's best to establish a strict routine and feed at the same time every day, and remove any uneaten food after about twenty minutes. This will keep food mess from hardening on the plate, keep pests away, and be better for your pet, too.

Apply Some Pet Design to Your Place

The best pet, the best equipment, even the best training, all fall short of the best solution—the simple logical process of building with pets in mind. A few hours and a few dollars spent on this will save you thousands of hours and dollars and a lot of unkind thoughts about your pets.

Prevention is the key. If the mess never happens, you've saved yourself the work. First, apply the following basic maintenance-lowering principles:

- *Seal or apply stain repellent to all raw surfaces, so stains can't get in and stay (see page 37).*

- *Keep animals on hard floors whenever possible, or install a stain-resistant or stain-proof carpet without a pad.*

- *Select wall coverings and paints that are moisture-proof and scrubbable.*

What else can you do to save cleaning time if you have animals in the house?

SIMPLIFY YOUR HOME

Get rid of the excess that complicates the cleaning effort. An animal is bound to disrupt a few things if a house is a maze of trinkets and decorations, so pet-proof the house just as you would kid-proof it.

- *Put small breakable things high on sturdy shelves.*

- *Minimize loose things such as pillows that can be disarranged.*

- *The fewer things on the floor, the better.*

- *Hang things up out of their reach. Pets, like children, are curious and sometimes bored. They'll experiment with anything that looks interesting, and may make a mess.*

GIVE THE ANIMAL HIS OWN PLACE

so he doesn't make ruins of yours. Concentrate your pet's living area whenever possible. Keep all his care needs there, or at least together, to save time and storage mess.

Also provide entertainment for your pets. If an animal has his own play area and toys, he's more likely to leave yours alone.

APPLY STRUCTURE DISCIPLINE

Anything that will close, spring back, reseal itself after use is an answer to a pet owner's prayers. Choosing short curtains so the cat can't swing on them is structure discipline. Closed doors are structure discipline. So are shelves too high to jump for, or stereo speakers mounted where they can't be scratched. If you don't want the animal in an area, structure things so he can't get in.

BUILD IN OR SUSPEND THINGS

whenever you can—shelves, appliances, tables, beds, bookshelves, and

other furniture. You'll eliminate cracks that collect hair and all those cozy little hiding places for your pet to take his "kill" and chew on it.

Attached furnishings won't allow a pet to disrupt them. Table lamps, for example, are one of pets' favorite things to knock over. But if you hang lamps from the ceiling or wall-mount them, they don't have to be dusted around, don't offer cords to be chewed, and give you more usable light from fewer fixtures. And they'll never get knocked over again.

You can also build in or suspend such things as doghouses, pet beds and playthings, food and water dishes, and shelves for pet supplies. Suspend a little basket on the wall so your pet can stick his head in and get his toys out, and then all his toys can be put back there when he's done. Or go a step further and train him to put his toys back!

INSTALL SURFACES THAT ENDURE

Hard, smooth, tough, nonabsorbent surfaces such as plastic laminate (Formica) or sealed brick or stone will help a lot in places such as the wall next to the litter box or the pet bed or beside the birdcage. Plastic laminate is also a good choice for tabletops, wall units, counters, bureaus, and the legs of furniture in pet territory. Slops and stains will wipe right off—laminate will repel almost anything and hold up to abuse. And it's available in an incredible variety of colors and finishes.

For the most part glass is a pet-proof material, too, because it only has to be washed. Animals can't scratch it, stain it, or chew on it. A mirror on a door, for example, will pet-proof it as well as serve human grooming purposes. Cats, especially, tend to avoid slick, or shiny, smooth surfaces.

SELECT LOW-MAINTENANCE FABRICS

for bedspreads, drapes, chairs, pillows, etc. Tightly woven, smooth-surfaced fabrics such as chintz are strong and durable and will resist a few little claw marks. And they're less likely to attract and hold hair.

If you have cats, try to tailor your furniture away from "nubby" or highly textured fabrics and wicker or other coarsely woven natural or synthetic fibers. Anything with a loose or open weave invites cats and dogs to pull at it, fiddle with it, claw or scratch it. And any filmy, delicate fabric can be shredded in seconds. Slick-surfaced fabrics are much less tempting to a scratcher.

WAX TO MINIMIZE PET MESS

The floor in a pet home needs extra protection. Waxing will protect hard-surface floors from spills, stains, grit, sand, and gravel, as well as the usual scuffs, heel marks, and dirt that would otherwise be ground into the surface. Wax or "floor finish" also keeps a floor, especially an unsealed one (see page 37), from absorbing odors and will even help protect it from scratching.

Even "no-wax" floors need a coat of floor finish or dressing at all times to protect and preserve their bright, glossy surface.

A good professional metal interlock wax from a janitorial supply store will last a lot longer than anything you buy in the supermarket. Its hard finish is self-polishing, so it doesn't need to be buffed or shined.

The Best Carpeting for Pets

is no carpeting, but we humans do love carpet. So the next best solution is to select all-synthetic fibers. Wool and cotton are absolute no-no's from a pet mess prevention standpoint; natural fibers absorb everything and that means odors and stains for sure. Nylon, Antron, polyester, and olefin loop pile, especially in "commercial grade" carpeting, are good choices for a carpet in heavy pet use areas. They resist staining, clean up easily, and hold up well under abrasion and wear. The best carpets for holding their color under the assault of stains are those in which the color is added as the synthetic fiber itself is being made—before it's formed into yarn. When the color is built right into the fiber this way, it won't easily fade.

Soil retardant such as 3M Carpet Protector or Pet Proof from Nilodor can make a big difference in carpet's ability to resist animal abuse. The protective film a retardant puts on the fibers (often fluorocarbon or Teflon) doesn't alter the feel or look of carpet, but it keeps stains and moisture from soaking in. If you're re-carpeting, be sure the carpet has a stain repellent applied at the mill, or look for the carpets made from the new synthetic materials that simply won't absorb a stain. These go by names like Stain Guard or Stain Blocker and even red punch won't penetrate these fibers, so anything from grape juice to urine or blood can be picked right up.

In rooms where pets spend a lot of time, it may be better for you to have an area rug than wall-to-wall carpet. With an area rug you can simply pick the rug up and apply a pet stain remover or bacteria/enzyme digester (see page 11) and then machine wash or dry clean the whole thing to get the smell and spot completely out.

Carpet tiles are another good idea for using in areas where pets live or spend a lot of time. They're available in textures from short loop to shag, they're easy to install (they're laid down exactly like hard floor tiles), and they look just like regular carpet once they're installed. But if an animal has an accident you can just pull up the whole 12" × 12" square to clean or replace it, to *completely* eliminate odor.

If you can't face life without wall-to-wall, give pet accidents less to soak into. This means choose the padless kind of carpet that's attached to the floor with contact cement. Thick padding under a carpet provides a perfect sponge for urine. And underneath the carpet, in pet use areas, concrete is the best surface—sealed, of course.

A textured or multilevel loop carpet in medium, variegated tones, or tweed will hide the most and a plush carpet with varied hues of the same basic color in it is next best for hiding dirt and animal hair. Deep shags are the hardest to clean and offer the snuggest home for fleas. Stick to tightly woven dense piles and, of course, synthetics like nylon.

If you match the color of your carpet, drapes, and furnishings to your pet (no, I'm not kidding), those dropped locks will show less.

CAMOUFLAGE WHENEVER YOU CAN

Choose colors and fabrics that won't show an occasional hair or crumb. Prints are better than plain solid colors, and lighter is better than darker. Animal hair will advertise itself on dark finishes, especially dark glossy finishes. Natural wood finishes, especially distressed wood, will hide little imperfections better than paint. Match your colors (furniture, drapes, and carpeting) to your animals and mess will show less.

Seal It Out

I've received many a blank look in my cleaning seminars when I counsel people to "seal" their floors, concrete, couches, carpets, corners, and fireplace brick. "Seal?" the audience wonders, "like sealing an envelope, or one of those creatures that claps its flippers when you toss it a fish?" I finally realized that a dramatic demonstration was in order.

Now I hold a piece of clear plexiglas over the knee of my crisp new suit and pour filthy water over it. Then I ask the audience why my suit isn't getting wet, dirty, and ruined. "Because," they yell

back, "there's a piece of plastic protecting it." That's what sealing basically does—it puts a transparent protective coating over a surface, a "membrane" finish that moisture can't penetrate.

I'm sure you can see the value of this where pets are concerned. Urine will soak into an unsealed surface and the odor from the residue will be reactivated every time the area gets damp or moist. Cleanup will require more chemicals and be five times harder. But if it's sealed, when the spray hits it won't soak in, stain, or be hard to clean off. With these surfaces, you can use water-based cleaners and deodorizers without qualms, to keep the area clean and free of odors. Sealing costs little and pays big, especially when it comes to ease of cleaning. And you may be surprised to learn how many different materials and surfaces around your house can be sealed.

Sealing can be done with many substances, most often with a varnishlike coating that's sprayed, brushed, rolled, mopped, or wiped on. Apply a sealer in two or three light coats, and let it dry in between, rather than one heavy one. And keep an eye on a sealed surface over time to make sure the sealing is still intact. If it begins to chip and wear off, it's time to smooth the surface, if necessary, and reapply.

Urethane sealers are great for wood and concrete floors. Acrylic (water-based) sealers can also be used on concrete, quarry tile, terrazzo, etc. Semi-gloss or gloss enamel paint will effectively seal walls or vertical structures such as posts. For brick and stone, a layer of low-luster clear acrylic or masonry sealer will be almost invisible, yet will prevent pet spraying, smoke, and oily hand or pawprints from staining your beautiful masonry surfaces.

Soil retardants are the greatest for anything made of fabric. They actually coat the fibers of the fabric, establishing a barrier against dirt and odor penetration. They also make the treated item easier to clean when it does need cleaning, because spills will bead up on the surface rather than soak in. (You still want to work as quickly as possible on urine stains, however, before the stain seeps, by sheer gravity, past the carpet fibers into the backing and pad.) Soil retardants will come off when you wash a fabric item, but you can re-treat the surface back into durability easily.

You can have a soil retardant applied at the mill or factory to large items like furniture or carpeting, usually for an optional charge. You can also get soil retardant at a supermarket or janitorial supply store to treat furnishings and objects you already own, but be sure they're cleaned well before you apply the retardant. There are even specialized retardants, such as Nilodor's Pet Proof, specially formulated to resist urine penetration.

The trigger-spray bottles of soil retardant are great for treating furniture, clothing, and small articles and surfaces like accessories. For carpeting, a Teflon and fluorocarbon soil retardant such as Carpet Guard or 3M Carpet Protector is what you need. Some of these, such as Carpet Guard, can be purchased in gallon jugs at a janitorial supply house and self-applied; others must be applied by a professional carpet cleaner.

After they're dry, soil-retardant treated surfaces are perfectly safe for your pets, but make sure you apply the product in a well-ventilated area away from your pets, and don't use the treated article until it dries.

CHAPTER 3.

House-breaking

The #1 Solution to the #1 Pet Cleaning Problem

The importance of thorough housebreaking cannot be overemphasized. Everything that makes dogs worthwhile, enjoyable companions is destroyed if they can't be trusted in the house.

—The American Kennel Club

There's no way around it—house-training can make or break your whole relationship with your pet. More dogs are abandoned for house-soiling problems than for any other reason. (We'll talk about housebreaking dogs here; the equally important house-training of cats is covered later in the chapter.)

We have some powerful forces on our side in the housebreaking process. Dogs are easy to train because their natural instincts fit right in with our house environment. Dogs never want to soil their den—foul where they sleep or eat—even a four-week-old puppy will stumble away from his box to urinate.

All we're essentially doing in house-breaking is teaching a dog to extend its den to include the entire house.

It's important to understand that housebreaking and paper-training are not the same thing. *Housebreaking* means a dog is never allowed to eliminate inside the house. *Paper-training* means the dog relieves himself inside the house, but only in a specific place that never changes, and on sheets of newspaper. (Dogs can be trained to use a litter box, just like a cat, and a box of shredded newspaper or even cat litter is actually a lot cleaner than sheets of newspaper on the floor.) If you have physical disabilities that make it hard to walk your dog, have a puppy that hasn't been immunized yet that you don't want to take out in the street, or some other good reason why you can't housebreak your dog, then paper-training may be the way to go. Otherwise, training your dog to defecate and urinate outside is usually preferable.

Not realizing that paper-training isn't a prelude to housebreaking, but an entirely separate and different training system, many people make the mistake of putting a puppy on newspaper inside the home and encouraging him to eliminate there. Then they teach him to go outside, but he continues to mess on the floor because that's how he was first trained. Don't confuse your dog this way. Choose one type of toilet training and stick with it. If you have a new puppy that you leave in a crate, playpen, or other confined area while you're gone during the day, you may need to use newspapers simply to protect the floor or absorb any accidents that occur while you're gone. Just don't praise him for using them—save that for when he relieves himself outside, to help eliminate his confusion about where you prefer him to go.

The basic ingredients of housebreaking are confining your pet in some manner during the training period, setting up a carefully planned feeding, watering, and walking schedule (and sticking with it, so your pet is conditioned to *regularity* of elimination), and giving your pet lots of praise when he does the right thing. Confinement, which is especially important during the parts of the housebreaking period when no one is home, can be accomplished by a dog crate, a puppy playpen, or a pet gate.

Confining in Cages and Crates

There are lots of good reasons to crate-train your dog. Whenever a dog is feeling stressed, ill, or just tired, he can go to his own little place and enjoy peace and quiet. When he's in his crate, he won't be able to get into trouble (that *you'll* have to clean up), so he's spared the anxiety and confusion of wrong behavior.

With a crate, a regular elimination routine can be quickly established, greatly reducing the likelihood of accidents. Your pet will have an easier time learning to control his bowels because a dog won't deposit his wastes in the area he considers his den—so he'll only relieve himself when you let him out of the crate.

Most people, when first advised to crate-train their pet, react with doubt and horror—"*What! Put my dog in a CAGE?* How cruel! I couldn't do it—and he'd hate me forever if I tried." Yet after he's chewed up the coffee table, scratched the walls, and wet on the dining room floor for the umpteenth time, many people who feel they could never

cage their pet see nothing wrong with punishing or abusing him, or giving him up to a pound or shelter where his chances of finding a new home are slim. Some people will even decide to dump the animal off somewhere to fend for itself—now that is cruelty. Actually, because the dog is instinctively a den animal who will very likely seek his own enclosed, protected space—under a bed, desk, shelf, table, etc.—*he* views the crate as a security blanket, a nice private sanctuary of his very own, a "bed with a door." The fact that the door can be shut bothers the owner far more than the dog.

Though crates are mostly used for dogs, a cat that is ill, destructive, or having problems with litter-training is a candidate for crating, too. Because cats don't take to crates as readily as dogs, first try the separate room confinement method. If this doesn't work, then try using a crate.

As animal behaviorist Gwen Bohnenkamp says, "When introducing your pet to a crate, den or confinement area, *go slowly*. Make the area a pleasant place to be. Spend time there with your pet. Don't just toss it in and walk away. Make it one of the pet's favorite places by giving it extra special attention, affection, and treats only when it is there. Start out by confining it for short periods, and gradually increase the time until you can leave it for several hours."

The wire cage type is best for home

use because it can be used covered or draped to create a cozy den, or uncovered for more vision and ventilation and to permit the dog to feel like part of the family while confined.

Wire cages are lightweight, and fold up for easy storage and portability. Some are slanted on one end to fit in station wagon or hatchback vehicles.

The better models are made of stainless steel or chrome-plated or epoxy-coated wire with a removable floor pan or tray. The unplated wire cages might cost less and do just as good a job of keeping the pet inside, but they're more susceptible to rust and can discolor the coat of light-colored animals.

Airline crates restrict a dog's vision more, although the door is usually made of wire, and there are wire windows or vents in the sides. But some dogs feel too vulnerable in a wire cage and prefer the

security of this more enclosed atmosphere. Airline crates are usually made of molded plastic, metal, fiberglass, or wood or a combination of these. Fiberglass is frowned upon as a crate material by some pet experts because of the danger posed by splinters if the dog chews on the crate. And the molded plastic crates are definitely susceptible to being chomped on, especially if you have a dog who already has a chewing problem.

Keep in mind that crating is *not* recommended to keep your dog confined and alone for hours on end while you're away at work, school, or wherever. But if you must make use of the crating technique for at least occasional extended periods, be sure to make up for the dog's time in the crate by giving him lots of exercise and freedom to be with you when you're home. If it's not too far

from where you work, go home at lunch-
time and take your dog for a short walk
to allow him to exercise and relieve
himself (if he's a puppy you probably
should give him something to eat, depending upon his housebreaking schedule). If you have a friendly neighbor
nearby who likes dogs, ask or hire him
to walk your dog for you during the day.
Or you could adjust your full-grown
pet's feeding schedule to one meal early
in the evening so he'll eliminate before
you go to bed, and the urge to go won't be
as great during the day while he's
crated inside. And when you're leaving
a dog in a crate, be sure you leave him
with some toys, water in a clip-on dish
that can't be spilled, and something to
sleep on.

CRATE CLEANING

The easiest way to get a crate thoroughly clean is to load it into the back of your
car—or, if you don't want the mess in
your car, in the back of a pickup truck—
and run it down to the do-it-yourself car
wash to give it a high-pressure spray
cleaning. If it needs to be sterilized or
has a lot of stubborn buildup, you could
even take it someplace that has a steam
pressure spray (the kind they clean mo-
tors with to make them look brand
new). Set the cage down on the floor
over the drain and they'll shoot it with a
hot grease-dissolving solution that will
loosen every bit of dirt and dried doo-
doo. The heat will not only kill the
germs but insure that the weld joints
(potential rust spots) dry quickly.

Or you can simply put the cage out on
the driveway, or sidewalk, or other hard
surface outdoors and hit it with a garden hose, a scrub brush, and some all-
purpose cleaning solution with a little
Nilodor Surface Deodorizer added, or
you can just use Nilodor Deodorizing
Cleaner.

Let the cleaning solution sit on there
for a few minutes—just don't let it dry—
then scrub or wipe it down with an aggressive brush or nylon pad to dislodge
the stuck-on stuff and then give it another quick shot of solution (after all,
the most time-consuming part—getting
set up—is already done. It'll only take
two minutes to soap and scrub it down
again). Now rinse it with the hose, and
if you want to disinfect, apply a Chlorasan solution and leave it on there for ten
minutes. Then rinse well again, and
slap or strike the cage with the palm of
your hand to shake off all the excess
moisture, so it won't dry slowly and
rust. Put it in the sun to speed up drying, if at all possible.

In between cage cleanings, go over
all the wire surfaces with a stiff-bristled
vacuum attachment. This may seem
unnecessary because you can't see anything on it, but trust me. There *is,* and
getting rid of all that dust and clinging
dirt and hair will keep things cleaner
and more sanitary.

MORE COMPLETE
INFORMATION

on crating can be found in *A Pet Owner's
Guide To The Dog Crate* by Nicki Mey-
er. For a free copy send a stamped, self-
addressed, business size envelope to:
The Nicki Meyer Educational Effort,
Inc., Dept. WD, 31 Davis Hill Road,
Weston, CT 06883.

For an explanation of how to use
crates and confinement to correct litter-
box problems in cats, as well as other behavior problems in cats and dogs, write
to Gwen Bohnenkamp, Animal Behavior Department, San Francisco SPCA,
2500 16th Street, San Francisco, CA
94103. A tax-deductible donation to the
San Francisco SPCA will be appreciated.

Declare Certain Parts of the House Off Limits

Even if your pet is completely house-trained, there may still be areas in your home where you'd like to establish his presence as *verboten*. Places like the bedroom, the nursery, or the room with the oriental rug, for example—to keep down the amount of shed fur, protect particularly valuable furnishings, or for the pet's own protection.

Set aside or designate areas in the house where your animal is allowed and not allowed—that way only those rooms have to be given the extra care animal cleaning requires. Whether the pet is house-trained yet or not, it's a good idea to pick a room for this purpose that has a hard floor—not carpet—so it'll be easy to clean up any accidents that do occur. This is why kitchens, bathrooms, and utility rooms are often a good choice. You also want good ventilation and some sunlight, if possible; not a dark, damp, dungeon-like area. If a dog is paper-trained, put newspapers in one corner, and be sure to leave a clean litter box when confining a cat. Put the pet's bed in the room with him, his favorite toy, and some food and water—depending on how long he'll have to stay in there. And see that there's nothing in there that he can damage or hurt himself with. This means, for example, that you don't want a place packed and cluttered with stuff, or full of sharp or fragile objects or chemicals and machinery.

The rooms animals do inhabit will have to be vacuumed a little more often, deodorized from time to time, and require a little more miscellaneous cleaning. But two rooms are easier than ten and your pet will be none the worse for it. A dog can be kept out of a room by training him or setting up a barrier, like a pet gate, but cats have a tendency to listen to everything you have to say about the subject, agree with you completely, and go inside anyway. When you're inside the forbidden room, keep the squirt bottle handy; otherwise, just keep the door closed.

A PET GATE

enables you to keep your pet in a particular part of the house without sealing him away behind a closed door. Isolating a dog alone in a room with the door closed can make a dog feel so cut off from the rest of the family that it freaks out and forgets its housetraining or scratches up the walls or door. Most adult dogs can be trained to respect a gate and not jump over it, and pet gates will keep puppies and sometimes kittens from venturing into other rooms. Cats tend to jump over these barriers with ease.

Most gates designed to serve as indoor barriers can be adjusted to fit standard-size doorways. Although child gates can be used, some of these leave enough space for a small pet to squeeze through, or worse, to get its head stuck. And wooden gates can be chewed into dangerous splinters. The metal or hard plastic gates made especially for pets are better since they have smaller openings, yet aren't completely opaque. (Pets like to at least see what's going on, even if they can't join in the action.) A cottage or dutch door with the top left open can also serve as a pet gate.

PLAYPENS

Young animals, just like young humans, can be kept in a playpen to keep them out of trouble and confine their messes to one place. This can be a wire exercise pen, a converted human playpen, or a playpen built especially for pets. Playpens are most often used for kittens, puppies, and small adult dogs, but they can be a nice place for your rabbit to frolic in, too.

If you're using a playpen for puppies, you can keep their bed, toys, food, and water right in there with them. They'll play and sleep on one side of the pen, and use the other side to relieve themselves. The tray on the bottom of the pan will keep the newspapers you lay down from touching the floor, so no odor will be transferred to the floor. This is a big help in avoiding later housebreaking problems.

Some playpens have a wire grate across the bottom about an inch above the floor to allow the droppings and urine to fall through to a newspaper-covered tray below. This keeps the pup's floor cleaner and drier, and prevents him from stepping in his own wastes.

Most exercise pens don't have trays in the bottom, so if you use a pen indoors you'll have to use plastic sheeting, several small trays, or a piece of sealed plywood to cover the floor—or be sure you put the pen on a sealed hard floor.

More Housebreaking How-To

Cleaning is actually critical to the success of house-training. A dog has a natural inclination to go again in places where he, or other dogs, has gone before. So if you don't clean up promptly and completely after accidents you're actually cueing him to a repeat performance. It's also important to remove any old urine or feces odors that may be found in the carpet, floors, or furnishings in your home from previous pets you've had, or even pets someone else had before you moved in. (More on exactly how to do this on page 66.)

If you paper-train, you should put a plastic sheet underneath the paper, or consider using the commercially available "piddle pads" to prevent urine from seeping through and leaving its odor on the floor. And of course, you never want to paper-train a dog on an absorbent surface—only on easy-to-clean surfaces like sheet vinyl or ceramic tile, so any urine or feces that leaks through the paper won't soak into the floor to become a scentmarker for the dog to return to later.

You also want to clean your pet's crate or bed or pen promptly if he happens to have a slip there—never let a puppy stay in a soiled bed or crate. The cleaner you keep your dog and his area, the harder he will work to keep from messing in your home. If you let your dog go for months without a bath, never groom him, and allow his bedding to become rank and odoriferous, you shouldn't be surprised if he decides, "Hey, why shouldn't I just dump in the middle of the carpet—with this mess, who'd even notice?"

Another important principle of housebreaking is not allowing your pet the chance to make mistakes in the first place. This means, for example, becoming alert to the subtle signs of "about to. . . ." Generally, when a dog has to relieve himself, he sniffs close to the ground and may whimper, whine, or make gagging noises, followed by squatting and elimination. With a young puppy, the time between the sniffs and squats might be very short, or he might not give any sign at all. So immediately after the pup wakes up, or right after he's eaten, or after you've been playing with him, you'll have to take him right to where you want him to go. (Don't drop him right outside the back door to do his duty. That's *not* where you want to get him in the habit of going.) Once he's relieved himself, praise him enthusiastically and he'll come to understand that relieving himself in the right place will make you happy, which is all dogs want their masters to be.

Don't expect your pet to be unfailingly housebroken until he's at least four months old—he simply won't have full and reliable control over the muscles involved in elimination until then. And don't pay attention to the old wives' tale about "rubbing your pet's nose in it to teach him a lesson." You won't teach him a lesson, but you will frighten and confuse him. (And maybe get him into the exasperating and hard-to-break habit of eating his own stools.) Unless you actually catch your pet in the act, attempts to "correct" housebreaking mistakes don't accomplish much.

There are lots of good books on housebreaking your dog, and the following are a few I especially recommend: *How to Housebreak Your Dog in 7 Days* by Shirlee Kalstone, *When Good Dogs Do Bad Things* by Mordecai Siegal and Matthew Margolis, and *The Evans Guide for Housetraining Your Dog* by Job Michael Evans.

Just remember that the more patience, effort, determination, persistence, and love you put into the few short weeks of housetraining your pet, the faster the training will take effect. And that means less piddle, poop, mess, odor, stain, aggravation and cleanup.

For Cats

Litter training is essential, but we can't take much credit for it. A cat's natural instinct is to dig a hole in the ground, do its duty in the hole, then cover it up. And the litter box, being the nearest thing to the soft earth of the outside and the most convenient place to exercise that instinct inside, is what they'll use, once they know where the box is. You can usually litter train a cat in about twenty seconds—the time it takes to introduce him to the litter box. Sometimes you might have to restrict a cat to a single room for a while to reduce the ground he has to cover to find the box and realize its function, but once he finds it, he'll use it.

A little praise when the initial duty is done right and a sharp clap and "No, no!" if puss chooses to go outside the box will help to keep the cat aware of the litter pan. A good time to introduce a kitten or new cat to the pan is right after eating a hearty meal—eating stimulates the bowels, and the chances for success are good.

The Best Boxes

The litter box is a simple concept, but there must be thousands of choices about how to set it up, where to put it,

Litter Unlimited

46

what litter to use, etc. You can go from totally primitive to Plush Flush. There are only a few basic principles to bear in mind for odor control and easy box maintenance, so you and your pet's personal opinion is very much to the point here.

WHAT KITTY LIKES . . . COUNTS

Nope, he isn't necessarily spoiled or finicky. Just like us, our pets feel comfortable with certain things and places over others. Our last cat might have loved and faithfully used a blue plastic litter pan with beet chip litter, but due to some inborn inclination or bad past experience, your new cat may be repulsed by it and refuse to go near it.

An important principle of success when it comes to choosing the type of box and litter to use is finding something your cat really likes. Cats won't do anything they don't want to do, and they especially won't use a potty not of their choosing, so don't get shook if your cat selects a stark open pan over the El Supremo heated toilet chamber.

DISHPANS

Len Waxman of Woodside, New York, has probably given litter pan maintenance more thorough study than any living human, and he maintains that the best and most perfect cat litter container is a kitchen dishpan. This is the standard 11x13-inch plastic pan with sides that are 6 or even 8 inches high, to hold down spillage and tracked out litter. (Unless you have a kitten, in which case you need a pan with sides no more than 5-7 inches high.)

A dishpan has built-in handles and is easy to carry, easy to clean, dump, and replace. Lots of folks get two of these since they're inexpensive. Then, if you're gone for awhile, if one gets to the

point where a cat won't piddle in it, he'll revert to the other and not the floor.

This is too small for a litter box, you say? It's plenty big enough for a cat to turn around in, yet small enough to make it likely that your pet will urinate against the side or in the corner of the pan. The advantage of this will be explained shortly. (If you'd like a guide that explains and illustrates every aspect of litter box management, with some real wit and cat wisdom along the way, you can get it by sending $5.00 along with your address to Len Waxman, 59-40 Queens Boulevard, Woodside, NY 11377 for a copy of *Preventing Litter Box Odor: The No-Frills Way*.)

BOXES WITH RIMS

have a wide lip all around the top that leans inward. This type of box is good for unneutered male cats because when the cat sprays, the rim keeps it from spraying out onto the walls and floor. This style of box also does a lot to prevent tracking.

COVERED LITTER BOXES

can help with the spraying problem too. They also help to hide the box and to keep mess down—you can be sure that the litter will stay in the box. And they do keep down odor to a degree—at least *outside* the box. The trouble is, they actually concentrate the odors inside the box, even to the point that kitty may be highly reluctant to use it, especially if you've neglected to clean it. The lid on covered boxes comes off and you should take it off to clean the litter regularly if you choose this style of box.

A covered box with a filter to absorb odor does a better job of keeping odor down than a covered box without a filter. The Boodabox, which has a charcoal filter built into the top, is a popular example of this style.

A TWO-LAYERED BOX WITH NONABSORBENT LITTER

lets urine seep down through the litter to be absorbed by a special odor-neutralizing paper you put beneath a grid or screen in the bottom of the box, or in a second separate pan beneath the top one. The Kitty Privy is one model of this type that's gotten good reviews from cat owners.

Whatever arrangement you choose, though, remember the first principle of design—keep it simple. If things are too elaborate and complicated they won't get used. If the box is hard to use, lift, carry, dump, or clean, your pet will delay using it and you'll delay or avoid cleaning it and the result will be odors and anger at the animal.

Creative Concealment

Do *you* ever pick the bathroom stall with the broken or missing door? No, you'll suffer and hold it awhile. And if you have to walk eight miles to the toilet, won't you just go quietly behind a bush?

Pets aren't that different from us, and their elimination drive is just as urgent. When you gotta go, you gotta go, and you don't want to climb, dig, hunt, and wait for a place forever. You want to be sure the box is handy and available to the cat at any hour of the day or night. Yet like us, cats have some modesty, too, so they appreciate a little privacy as well as convenience. Don't put it near the cat's feeding area or in a noisy or heavily trafficked spot. A place with a little concealment is best. Just make sure the box is set on a hard nonabsorbent surface such as ceramic tile or seamless vinyl, otherwise any litter box accidents or overshots that occur will install "go here again" signals in the carpet.

Generally your pet will use the box where you put it, but some cats will select their own spot and go there. Remember: What kitty likes counts. Move the litter box to that spot. On the other hand, don't keep switching the location of the litter box, or you may confuse your cat and up the accident ratio. And if you have a large house, a number of cats, or an older cat who can't get around as easily as he once did, consider placing litter pans in more than one location.

An open box is surely the cheapest and simplest to service and perhaps even the most attractive to a cat, but it isn't the sort of thing a guest (or any of us for that matter) cares to gaze upon. The available space in every home differs, of course, but here are a couple of good places to consider when it comes to concealment.

THE BATHTUB OR SHOWER

What better place to hide the box—you can just pull the shower curtain or shut the shower door. It's close to the toilet, too, for quick disposal of solid wastes. And since the tub has a hard waterproof surface and a built-in water supply, it's one of the easiest places in the house to clean and disinfect. Bathrooms have built-in fans to dissipate odor, too.

Place a heavy towel in the bottom of the tub or on the floor of the shower and set the litter box in the middle of it. The toweling should extend at least four inches beyond the sides of the box to protect the bottom of the tub or shower and give your pet some traction on the slick tub surface. This will also serve as a little doormat to collect any litter that may have clung to your cat's paws during a visit to the box. Then when you're servicing the pan, you simply lift the towel up and dump any loose litter back into the pan.

CAT IN THE CUPBOARD

Inside a lower cupboard can be a good place for the litter box, too, if you can train your cat to open the door (and all smart cat owners claim they can). When the cat needs to go, it just paws open the door and uses the box. The advantage of this location is again concealment. Just be sure the cupboard has a latch a cat can handle (or install a pet door in the cupboard door, if you don't mind sacrificing it). But don't use a kitchen cupboard for this, because a litter box can carry harmful E. coli bacteria, so you don't want it anywhere near where you prepare food. And you'll want to disinfect a cupboard used for this purpose regularly.

The following are some cupboard possibilities:

- *In a closet or pantry with the door ajar (if you're in the giddy position of having a closet to spare for the purpose).*

- *In the garage, with a pet door or passageway to it from the house. It's discreet, and convenient to the garbage can.*

- *Take out the large bottom drawer of a piece of furniture and replace it with the box, then string a little curtain across the front.*

- *Put the box on the bottom shelf of built-in floor-to-ceiling shelves, again, with a curtain across the front of the shelf.*

- *You could even construct a square or rectangular bottomless cabinet of sealed stained plywood, with a cat-size entryway in one side.*

- *There are attractive "privacy screens" and even fabric tent coverings commercially available for a box that has to be in a more conspicuous spot, or you could devise your own.*

Get Down to the Real Kitty-Gritty

Shredded newspapers, sand, dirt, sawdust, wood shavings, and probably twenty other things could be used in a pinch, but it costs a dollar less to go first class, especially when it comes to cat litter. Soggy newspaper, for example, inks up an animal's feet and cats don't like standing on it. A lot of things will work, but what works best and is inexpensive, easy to store, and easy to find at the corner market? Plain old commercial cat litter. If you use a lot of litter, you can buy it in bulk (50-pound bags).

Good commercial litters (most of them are clay-based) absorb and hold the liquids and solids of cat waste efficiently, and they do a far better job of minimizing odor than shredded paper, dirt, or wood shavings. Look for a brand that isn't excessively dusty, and always pour litter slowly to keep down dust. The sharp little silicate or clay particles of litter dust aren't good for lungs or allergies, cat or human.

Certain cats won't use some of the best litter, so it might take a brand or two to find out what they like. When you find it, use it.

If you do go for a box filled with shredded paper, which might be needed for a cat's tender front feet in the first weeks following a declawing operation, or for a pet other than a cat using a litter box, don't use magazine paper—most of it is too slick and nonabsorbent. Don't make the strips too wide, and be sure to remove the soiled paper right after each use, or at least daily.

How much litter you put in the pan is also important. Too much and the cat sinks in it, not enough and he can't exercise his "bury my droppings" instinct. You don't want more than three inches

in there and the truly perfect depth, according to Mr. Waxman, is just one inch. In general, underfilling is better than overfilling—it means less kicked-out and wasted litter.

You'll find a variety of plastic litter box liners available, including those with attached drawstrings and some that snap right into a rim specially constructed to hold the liner in place (a worthwhile feature, since liners tend to slip down off the sides). A box liner would seem to be an advantage when box-dumping time rolls around, but they're often clawed through by kitty as he digs, and then urine seeps under the liner and the box smells worse than ever.

DEODORIZED LITTER OR LITTER DEODORIZERS

can extend the time between litter box cleanings—you can either buy a deodorized product or add your own deodorizer to plain litter. Some deodorized litters contain chemicals and fragrances that actually repel cats, forcing them to use some other handy corner of the house.

And in a covered box, the scent of the litter deodorizer itself is likely to build up to the point that your pet refuses to go inside. Of the litters made of materials that are supposed to be odor-masking or counteracting in themselves, cedar chip litter is tolerated better by most cats than alfalfa-pellet litter, for example. But cedar litter is so light it not only gets tracked out but sticks to the cat and gets carried all over the house. And a dropped chip, smelling of litter box as it does, can cue a cat to go elsewhere than the box.

It's often easier on the pet and on the pocketbook to buy plain clay litter and add your own odor counteractant. The overwhelming favorite of experienced cat owners in this category is plain old baking soda. Eighty percent of the respondents to a recent *Cat Fancy* survey, for example, indicated that they had better results with baking soda than with chemical treatments of any kind. When you're setting up or changing the box, mix in one part baking soda to three parts litter, and put a layer of soda on the very bottom of the box, too. If you do want to mix in commercial deodorizer, a bacteria/enzyme type like Outright Odor Eliminator (the powdered type made especially for litter pans) is probably the best.

Keeping the box clean is the great odor-conquering secret—the precise type of litter you use, exactly where you put the pan, the available ventilation, etc. help a little but *cleaning out the box often* is the real secret. The more boxes you have in the house, and the more cats using them, the more important this is.

Litter Box Cleaning

The real experts again go for simplicity. The litter box rakes and slotted scoops do a very efficient job of removing feces, if you have to go with a single tool, the old faithful *un*slotted metal serving spoon or the like is the very best because it picks up urine-soaked clumps of litter or loose stools completely, so that nothing falls through the slots to get mixed back down with the clean litter and smell up the box.

The big question is *how often* should you clean the box? This varies according to the inclinations of the owner and the number and nature of the cats using it and perhaps, too, on where you keep the box. "Pan out" the solid wastes at least daily, then change the litter completely, and wash and disinfect the container about once a week. (If you don't disinfect, at least use as hot a rinse water as you can manage when you clean it.) This is for a one-cat situation; if the box is used by more than one you're back in the realm of personal appraisal. Some cats are fussy and won't use a "soiled several times" place, so you have no choice but to service it more often or get a mess on your floor.

Remember that cats have much keener noses than we do, so it might look and smell okay to us but be beyond the pale to our pet. Many "litter box managers" make the mistake of assuming that if they scoop out the solids regularly, they've done all they can to keep odor down between full-scale cleanings. But it's the urine that creates that awful ammonia-like stench too often thought of as the trademark of a cat household. You want to remove the urine daily, too, or the sooner the better. Tilt the box gently to one side and any urine deposits will stand out as darkened masses of wet litter that stick to the side or bottom of the pan. Slide a spoon or flat scoop carefully under the clump and try to remove it intact if at all possible. Corner or side clumps are much easier to remove without breaking than clumps deposited in the middle, hence the advantage of a smaller

pan. If you do break a clump, don't mix it with the remaining clean litter; this is one of the best ways to *insure* a smelly box. If the box contains both urine and feces, try to ferret out and remove all the fragile urine clumps first, to avoid broken clumps that contaminate and smell up the pan. Do your daily waste-panning with the box right up against the toilet, if possible, to keep spills down.

GRAND CENTRAL LITTER BOX

If you have only one cat, the "spoon and corner" technique should work well for you, but a multiple-cat household calls for a somewhat different approach. A single cat, fed once or twice a day, will usually deposit his feces one to three times per day, although he may urinate more often, especially if he has access to water all day. If you use the tall dish-pan-style litter box, the cat will usually urinate in one of the four corners, and if he's not too vigorous in his burying he won't disturb the urine clump. This makes it easy for you to pick out clumps with your spoon and dispose of them. But in a multiple-cat household, this "clump-picking" is pretty hard to do because there's just no way to keep the clumps unscrambled. Those cats will be competing for clean, dry waste space, and like little furry prospectors they're going to dig until they hit paydirt. If you have only two cats, you may be able to get around the problem by giving each animal his own box, but that's still no guarantee they won't decide to switch off. So for a multiple-cat household get yourself a good litter scoop, for example, Sun Hill's Maxi Litter Scoop, which allows you to sift a lot of litter at a time, and has an elevated handle to keep your hand above it all. Scoop out the feces every day, and don't worry about stirring up the litter since the urine clumps will probably be broken up anyway. But this means you'll want to change the litter and wash the box at least twice a week to keep down the urine odor.

How much odor there is and whether or not your pet uses the box depends more on how regularly you service it than any other single factor. If it isn't left, it won't smell and you're much less likely to have "accidents" anywhere in the house. Prompt litter box cleanout also keeps worm eggs and other parasites in the stool from reaching the infective stage.

To keep down germs and odor, every week, mop the floor under and around the box with a deodorizing cleaner solution and rinse. And from time to time apply a Chlorasan solution to the area: leave the solution on for five to ten minutes, then rinse it off with a mop dampened in clean water.

Don't forget to wash your hands well after handling or changing the pan. And do take note of any changes in your cat's toilet habits, such as straining, constipation, or diarrhea. These can be symptoms of a wide variety of illnesses. If they don't clear up soon, consult your vet, of course.

Can You Really Toilet-Train Your Cat?

If you've wondered about the "cat toilet training products" that are advertised—yes, they do work. You don't even need to buy a kit, although they do have the advantage of being made specifically for the purpose. What cat toilet training basically does is teach the cat to transfer his litter box talents, in gradual steps, to a higher and rather peculiar litter box. Most of the kits have some sort of plastic liner or other device that fits over or below the toilet seat and holds a small amount of litter and per-

haps a catnip attractant. You gradually adjust kitty to less litter and more open space, as you guide him through the interim stages. It's that exquisite feline sense of balance and the fact that cats normally excrete in a squatting position that makes this all possible.

Toilet training is fine for individual cats, but not every cat will do it. If you've instituted a training program and he seems reluctant, don't force your pet. And if you have four or five cats in the house the feces may tend to clog up the drain, since cats haven't yet learned to flush. But they can be toilet trained. It's not inhumane, it's not silly, and it's not hard to do. It eliminates litter box odors and the chores of box maintenance and saves all that money shelled out for litter, too. If you're interested, here are some manufacturers who can sell you a kit that contains all the instruction you need.

Kitty Commode, L. R. Hammond Co., P.O. Box 3526, Riverside, CA 92509. (This device is almost like a cat-tailored version of a child's potty chair—it gives the cat more secure seating and can also be used off the toilet, on a special base to which you add water and an antibacterial agent.)

Cat Can: The Tabby Toilet Trainer, Shippan Distributors, Inc., 176 Ocean Drive West, Stanford, CT 06902 (203)356-1066.

Kitty Whiz Transfer System, The Cat's Whiskers, 1104 N.W. 30th, Oklahoma City, OK 73118 (405)524-5610.

TOILET TRAINING YOUR CAT WITHOUT A KIT

Start by putting the litter box on the toilet (make sure the lid is down), and put the cat up there in the box so he realizes it's been moved from the regular spot. If he doesn't seem to want to use it in this new location, figure out when he ordinarily uses the box (usually after his meal), then put him inside the bathroom and close the door at just that time. After you're pretty sure he's used the box, let him out. If you put fresh litter in the box before letting the cat in, you can be sure of whether he's used it or not.

Once he gets used to this, begin putting the box on the toilet with the lid up, so the box is sitting on the toilet seat. (To a cat, this shouldn't make any difference.)

After a few days of this, take a round or oval disposable aluminum roasting pan (make sure it's sturdy enough that it won't bend and fall into the toilet) or a plastic dishpan that will fit inside the hole in the seat without falling through, and set it inside the seat. Put about ¼ inch of litter inside, and put the litter-filled pan inside the toilet when it's your cat's regular potty time. This will probably seem a little unusual to your pet, but since there's litter inside he should go for it. (Give him some peace and quiet for this initial transition period.)

By now your cat should start stand-

ing on the toilet seat when he goes, hanging his rear over the pan. After you get him used to going this way (hopefully within a few days), cut a small hole about 2 inches in diameter in the middle of the pan, and start decreasing the amount of litter inside. A couple of days later decrease the litter even more and increase the size of the hole by another inch or two. After a week you should be down to no litter in the pan and a hole large enough so there's really nothing inside for the cat to scratch except water down below. If you've got your pet to this point, you're finished with training.

If you do opt for toilet training, a solid plastic seat is better than a painted wood or padded one because cats may scratch a little after using the toilet, as a reflex. For this same reason, a Formica, glass plate, or other scratch-resistant surface on the wall closest to the toilet might not be a bad idea. And if kitty does use the toilet, wipe the top and bottom of the seat every week with Chlorasan solution after you do your regular toilet cleaning. Leave the solution on for five or ten minutes, then wipe it off with a cloth moistened in clean water.

Spraying

Even perfectly house-trained animals will spray. Animals use urine (and for that matter, feces) to communicate with other animals, to leave their scent on places and things to give other animals a variety of different messages. In general, if a urine stain is on a vertical surface, it's no "accident"—it was the intentional urination we call spraying when male cats do it, and "leglifting," in dogs. Male cats and dogs are the most notorious for spraying, but females will sometimes spray, especially when they're in heat.

A sprayer's targets are usually the most conspicuous objects in a room—things like doors, stereo speakers and furniture, or just below or on windows. If you don't act fast on a spray spot, you'll have permanent staining of absorbent surfaces. And if you don't remove all trace of the odor your pet will be encouraged to christen the spot again. Spraying poses a safety hazard, too: pets can spray on and in things (such as wall sockets, electric heaters, or even the Christmas tree) and get a serious electrical shock.

Neutering And Spaying—The #1 Solution for Spraying

The majority of spraying is done by unneutered animals. Having your pet altered will give you a 90 percent or better chance of eliminating spraying if he's a cat, and at least 70 percent if he's a dog. Usually your pet will stop spraying within several weeks after the operation, as soon as the male hormones have faded from his system. But don't wait until he's old enough to have firmly established "marking" habits or he'll still spray after neutering. The main reason neutering isn't always as effective in eliminating spraying in dogs is that they're more likely to continue to spray out of pure habit after the hormonal impulse is gone. You don't want to have a cat or dog neutered before he's at least six months old, but as soon after that as you see any sign of an inclination to leglift or go outside the box, he's ready.

If spraying persists even after neutering, consult your vet or an animal behaviorist. She may suggest treating your pet with synthetic female hormone or anti-anxiety drugs for awhile to alter his behavior.

The spaying and neutering procedures are safe, and unless you have a choice purebred and intend to become a professional breeder, there's no good reason *not* to have it done.

Cats and dogs that are spayed or neutered are healthier, happier, more affectionate, tend to live longer, and don't contribute to the tragedy of pet overpopulation. Any one of these is a good enough reason to alter, but here's a reason most people never think of: it makes it easier to keep your home *clean!*

A few more benefits of spaying and neutering:

- *Your pet will be more trainable, because he's less distracted.*

- *He'll be more content to stay home (and you won't have to worry about him roaming all over and getting hurt or worse).*

- *He'll be gentler and less aggressive.*

- *He'll urinate less frequently and forget his toilet training less frequently.*

- *He won't try to mount your boss's leg or stick his nose where he shouldn't.*

- *He'll also be less susceptible to prostate trouble and testicle tumors.*

Depending upon where you live and where you go to have it done, spaying can cost you anywhere between $50 and $175 for female dogs (size, weight, and whether she's pregnant at the time all figure into the price), $50 to $150 for spaying female cats, and from $40 to $150 for neutering male cats and dogs.

But humane organizations in many areas have programs that provide lower cost spaying and neutering services for those who might not be able to afford it otherwise. Check with your city's municipal shelter or your local humane society for information.

There is also an organization called Friends of Animals, 1 Pine Street, Neptune, NJ 07753, that will help you get your pet spayed or neutered for a very reasonable price. More than 800 veterinarians in forty-six states belong to the Friends of Animals spaying and neutering program, and you can write the organization or call their toll-free number (800/631-2212) for more information. They'll send you a list of participating veterinarians and a form you fill out and send back to them, along with the payment. Depending on where you live, this will bring spaying costs down to about $30 for a female cat and about $45 for a female dog, and the neutering cost to only about $16 for a male cat and $30 for a male dog. They'll send you back a certificate to take to the participating vet near you, and it covers not only the spaying or neutering, but also having your pet examined and inoculated, an overnight stay after the operation if it's called for, and the removal of the stitches later. Even if your female cat or dog is pregnant, there's no extra charge. And this program isn't just for those who can't afford it—it's for anyone, rich, poor, or in between.

Solution #2: Training

The Scat bottle, good as it is elsewhere (see page 16), doesn't seem to work for most owners trying to break their pet of spraying. Your pet can very easily spray and say good day before you even notice. And if you don't correct a pet immediately (this means within a *half second* of the behavior) it does no good—even a few seconds later is too late. For this same reason paper-whacking or the like won't work—you simply can't do it fast enough.

You might be able to yell *"No"* or *"Stop"* fast enough, clap your hands, toss a shake can, or honk a compressed air horn, especially if you keep a sharp eye out for the symptoms of "about to spray": your cat backing up to something with a raised, twitching tail or a set of short funny little steps, or your dog raising his leg.

You can also try the diversion approach when you see the signs: toss him a toy, start a lively game with him, pick him up and pet him, or carry him somewhere else.

As animal behaviorist Gwen Bohnenkamp points out, "You can actually teach a dog not to mark inside. Nothing will entice a male dog to urinate more than the smell or presence of another dog's urine. Using cotton balls, soak up some urine from another dog and save them in the freezer in a plastic bag. Tack a half-dozen of the urine-soaked cotton balls to a post outside and let your dog discover them. As soon as he sniffs and squirts, praise and reward him. Repeat this until you know he understands how delighted you are with his marking outside.

"Then find a safe location indoors and tack one of the cotton balls there. Watch your dog very closely. As soon as he begins to sniff and position himself to lift his leg—but before he actually urinates—shout 'No! Bad dog! Outside, outside, outside' and chase him outdoors. Once outside, he'll find the post where you've previously tacked the cotton balls. When he urinates on them, praise him profusely. In just a few seconds, he's learned that trying to mark indoors makes you angry, but marking outdoors makes you very happy and he gets praised for it. (It's a good idea to have previously taught your dog what the word 'outside' means.)"

CONFINEMENT

can be used to break a dog or cat of spraying in the house. Confine the sprayer to a small room with washable

55

surfaces and a hard floor, or to a crate. If he's a cat, put the litter box in there with him, make sure he uses it, and after he does, praise him, let him out, and watch his every move. If you see the slightest sign of about-to-spray, put him back in and don't let him out until he uses the box. If he's a dog, be sure to take him outside to urinate regularly and again, never let him out of confinement without a sharp eye on him.

Don't leave a sprayer in the process of retraining home alone unless he's confined, and don't be too quick to decide that he's got the idea. Don't give him the run of the house until he's stopped urinating in the wrong places for several weeks running.

Prevent

If you have a cat that sprays, keep the litter box extra clean so your pet has no excuse to avoid it. And don't ever attempt to correct your pet while he's in the litter box—it could make him avoid it entirely.

Be sure to place the litter box well away from walls or absorbent surfaces. Get one of the boxes with a high rim that will keep your pet from spraying out of the box. Or consider a covered box with a charcoal filter. There's one that's guaranteed to be spray-proof: the Kitti Potti from Haugen Pet Products of Ann Arbor, MI.

Since spraying is often repeated in the same places, you can move your pet's food or water dish or bed to that very spot, and keep it there until the spraying ceases in that location, since pets never want to soil where they sleep or eat. (This strategy might be called fighting one pet instinct with another.)

Don't leave things that wouldn't survive a spray session sitting exposed on low shelves, etc. For instance, don't leave clothing draped over couches, chairs, or bedsteads or you might have a very unwelcome surprise when you go to gussy up for the grand opening.

If a favorite spraying spot is on a piece of upholstered furniture, you can attach a matching piece of upholstered fabric over the spot and remove it to clean as necessary.

If the sight of other cats outdoors is causing the spraying, draw the drapes or install blinds or shutters. It will sometimes reduce or prevent spraying indoors if you let your cat outside briefly to exercise the spraying instinct.

If your male dog isn't neutered, don't bring him along while visiting, especially to a home with other pets. His urge to leave his calling card will be nothing less than overwhelming and the visitee will be less than happy with the result.

Clean It Up

Although pets can and will spray almost anything (including strangers' legs, other pets, and food), most of them will spray in the same area, spot, or place over and over—so cleaning it can actually be easy, as long as you seal the area.

This simply means applying a finish to the surface that moisture can't penetrate (see page 37). Then when the spray hits, it won't soak in, stain, or be hard to clean. Spraying can be quickly and easily cleaned off things and won't damage them if they have a slick protective surface. You might want to seal the basement walls, up to a height of about three or four feet, if a spraying pet spends a lot of time there.

You can locate unsuspected spray spots on furniture and baseboards, especially, by darkening the room and shining a flashlight on the floor so the light bounces upward. The spray will show up as shiny streaks.

On hard or sealed surfaces:

1. *Spray the spot with your spray bottle of deodorizing cleaner or all-purpose cleaner with some surface deodorizer added.*

2. *Let the solution sit on the surface for ten seconds or so.*

3. *Wipe it off with a paper towel and throw the towel away.*

4. *Spray it again quickly and wipe the area off thoroughly with a sponge or damp cloth.*

5. *As a final touch, you can spray the area with Chlorasan solution and let it dry on there, to inhibit the growth of bacteria.*

For spray stains on carpeting, upholstery, or other absorbent surfaces, be sure to follow the directions for removal of fresh or old urine stains on page 63. Fresh stains can usually be treated with a chemical deodorizer/cleaner, but aged spray stains will call for a bacteria/enzyme product.

Blood Stains

There are two good things about blood cleanup: 1) red is easy to see and so we usually catch bloodstains quickly, and 2) fresh blood is a fairly easy stain to remove. The bad news is that dried bloodstains are one of the tougher things to get out, especially if "set" by heat (as in a clothes dryer).

For fresh stains, always use cold water. Wet a cloth or sponge with cold water and blot the spot: wet and blot, wet and blot. I always prefer using a white cloth for stain removal because you can immediately see whether or not the fabric you're treating is colorfast.

The absolute best blood remover is plain old household ammonia. Make a solution of three tablespoons of ammonia to a gallon of cool water, and, after you've blotted with cold water, blot with the ammonia solution and the stain will come out. Rinse with vinegar to reduce the alkalinity left in the area, then rinse with water.

If the article or material you're trying to get the stain out of is white and a slight stain is left, you might try rust remover. Bleach it with a 3 to 5 percent solution of hydrogen peroxide as a last resort.

If the bloodstain is old and really set, soak it with a bacteria/enzyme digester (see page 11).

Pet Potty Detail

I remember the shock I suffered as a boy when I heard that Roy Rogers's beautiful palomino Trigger did it right on the stage in front of ten thousand fans. How could he, a famous and respectable horse, do that to Roy? I finally realized the answer was simple—the horse did it because it was the most natural thing in the world for him to do. And it was equally natural and straightforward for Roy to clean it up.

It's hard to face in a polite society, but animals do have to go . . . so we have to pick up, rake up, mop up, blot up, scoop up, scrape up, and shovel. But on the walk or in the backyard, scoop law or not, we all seem a little reluctant about this particular cleaning duty. The fact is, when it comes to the pet potty detail the secret isn't technique *or* equipment—it's *attitude*.

You can't prevent the act itself, but you can make pickup and disposal as easy as possible and control *where* they do it. Animals have to go somewhere, so wouldn't it be better to create a place for it than to have the yard and the landscape littered at will?

Set aside a certain part of the yard for the purpose. Then make a concrete pad, 3x3-foot or so, depending on the size of your dog. Slope the concrete in toward the center from the edges, and put a drain hole filled with gravel in the middle. Then you can easily scoop the droppings off the concrete surface and flush it off with a hose. Or cover a similar area with four inches of gravel. You can sur-round the area with bushes or shrubs to screen off the area and to give your pet a little privacy.

Then take your pet to the potty area when he needs to go (put some of his droppings there to encourage him to start using it if you need to), and praise him when he does. Pet stores have chemicals that will help attract a dog to a "potty post" while you train him.

Dogs actually prefer to eliminate in the same spot repeatedly—as long as it's kept clean. (If it *isn't*, they'll refuse to go there.) You want to pick up the droppings in the pet potty area—or the whole yard, if you let your dog go anywhere in the yard—very regularly anyway, preferably daily. It will look better and restore the joy of lawn rolling, plus cut down the chances of transmitting a lot of diseases and parasites. You can just scoop up the droppings and dump them down the toilet or in the trash (if your city code allows it), or install a waste digester, as described below.

You'll also want to deodorize a cement or gravel pet toilet area with bacteria/enzyme solution at least once a month, and disinfect it periodically.

Whatever you do, don't put dog droppings in an ordinary garden compost pile. Dog and cat droppings don't have the same value as fertilizer as the manure of herbivores, and they may carry parasites and disease germs to your garden soil, and attract wandering pets or wild animals to the pile.

Install a Waste Digester in Your Backyard

This is sort of like a septic system specifically for dogs. It's a cylindrical or pyramid-shaped container that's buried in the ground; you add a culture of harmless live bacteria to it and they produce enzymes that decompose and liquefy the stools so they can be absorbed into the earth. The only hitch is that when the temperature drops below 40° F, the enzymes slow down or stop functioning. This is one of the reasons the digester is set into the ground, because under the earth it's a constant 55° except in northern climates, where the top two feet or so freeze hard as rock.

A pyramid digester

A pair of digesters made from bell tiles

One way to get around this is to have two digesters and put the droppings in one all winter until the weather warms up in the spring, then gradually transfer them from the full digester to the empty one. An additional advantage is that in warmer weather two digesters can actually digest as much as three could if you alternate between them. If you install a digester below the frost line, it'll work all winter.

The best-known brand of enzyme digester is Lim'nate—a one-pound box will last a one or two-dog household about a year and costs less than $5. Outright Pet Odor Eliminator is a bacteria/enzyme product that also works very well for the purpose. These digesters can also be used to be sure pet stools don't clog up your human septic system, if you regularly dump pet waste in the toilet.

Many pet-supply distributors or feed or pet stores have metal or plastic stool digesters available, often complete with a scooper and a starter supply of enzyme. The Doggie Dooley is one of the better-known brands. You can also build your own from a ten-inch bell tile

or steel drum (*not* one previously used for insecticide or other toxic substances). Or you can dig a pit or construct an above ground box that serves the same purpose—the makers of Lim'nate will provide the instructions. All of these need a secure fly-proof cover. For any of these, you simply scoop the droppings up, drop them into the digester, and add more water and bacteria culture from time to time.

You want to install a digester away from wells and septic tanks, in a spot that has good drainage. You also want to make sure that the digester never dries out, that there's always enough solution in there to keep the stools semi-moist. On the other hand, don't add more water than the enzyme directions call for, or more solution than needed to just moisten the droppings, or you'll

A digester made from a bell tile and a steel drum.

lower the efficiency of the digester. You also don't want to add strong chemicals to the digester, or you'll kill the bacteria that produce the enzymes.

Teach Your Dog to Eliminate on Command

Training can be an excellent solution to the pet potty detail, too, but like potty-training kids it does take a little time and patience. The purpose of this book isn't to describe training techniques in detail, but *You Can Teach Your Dog to Eliminate on Command* by Dr. Marjorie Smith, available from Smith-Sager Publications, P.O. Box 1008, Friday Harbor, WA 98250, will teach you every nuance of accomplishing what might sound like the dog walker's impossible dream—getting your pet to go exactly *where* you want him to go, *when* you want him to. The animal experts agree that the concept is sound and even go so far as to say that it's ridiculously easy to accomplish. You can train any dog six weeks or older to PPC—"piddle and poop on command"—at the sound of a (carefully chosen) trigger word, and the total training time you'll have to spend doing it is less than ten minutes a week.

This technique will insure that you walk your dog, instead of him walking you. When most people walk their dogs, as soon as the animal eliminates he's taken home. After a while the dog probably begins to think, "Hey, if I can hold it in for a while, then she'll have to take me walking all over"—so you end up walking for what seems like forever. After you've taught your dog to eliminate on command, you can see that he relieves himself before the walk begins. Then you take him for his walk (that's his reward for eliminating on your command), and *you're* in control of how long you want the walk to last.

Elimination on command also means that you can assure a prompt "duty" on cold and rainy nights, or when you have to leave soon for somewhere. It also solves the problem of poop pickup in public places. You can see that your pet goes in the area you've set aside as the pet toilet, before you take him out on the town.

For More Scoopable Stools

The scooper's nightmare known as loose stools can be caused by a sudden change in diet, a high-fat diet, disease, parasites, or stress and excitement, just to name a few. Loose stools are a sign that something's amiss; if they last longer than a few days, take the dog to a vet.

High-quality, nutritionally dense dog food such as Science Diet, Eukanuba, or Iams creates firmer and smaller stools that are easier to pick up and don't leave messy residue when you do. A diet of $2/3$ ordinary name-brand dry dog food and $1/3$ canned food will also produce eminently scoopable stools.

If you do have to scoop a loose stool, throw some absorbent material on it so it can be picked up more easily. You can use deodorizing absorbent—the stuff you put on the garage floor to absorb grease, cat litter, or even dirt if nothing else is available—anything that will absorb and stiffen the mess so it can be scooped.

You can also use the newspaper technique. Slip a sheet of newspaper under your pet when he squats and try to position the paper so that he dumps in the middle of it, then fold the corners in and slip the paper inside an opaque plastic bag. This way, it there aren't any garbage cans close by, it's easy to carry until you find one. Presto, the mess is up—no runs, no drips, no errors.

CHAPTER **4.**

In Case of Accident...

In thirty years of professional service, my crews have cleaned up everything from suicides to skunk spray to smoke and fire damage. But some of the very worst messes we ever faced were the places that pets had been allowed to run wild in a house or apartment.

"Accidents" and odors are the two main reasons people give up their pets, and after my experiences cleaning up abused homes, I can understand the urge to abandon a situation like that. For the most part, though, we're not talking about such a totally out of control situation (caused, incidentally, by the owners, not the pets), we're dealing with the occasional incident. Even the best-trained pet will have an accident from time to time. If we forget to let Fifi out before we go shopping, or fail to keep the litter box clean and appealing, we may force a normally well-behaved pet to seek relief on forbidden ground. And occasionally an animal may eat something that doesn't quite agree, and have

a bout of vomiting or diarrhea. These are pure and simple accidents.

A different type of accident is the one where the animal knows a certain behavior is unacceptable, but for emotional reasons, as it were, does it anyway. A new pet or a new baby in the house, a new animal in the neighborhood, or any situation that produces anxiety, for example, may cause a pet to temporarily forget its training. Many a pet will make messes when frustrated, unhappy, or lonely. This type of temporary lapse, while certainly not fun for you, can usually be handled with a little re-education and some patience while you track down the reason for the strange behavior.

In the case of a normally well-behaved animal who has a slip for reasons he can't control, simply clean up the mess without getting upset at the animal, try to figure out the cause of the problem—and remove it. The same is true of accidents caused by psychological stresses on your pet, although rooting out the problem here and treating it is a little more involved. Many of these types of behavior and their solutions are covered under the individual topics elsewhere in this book. And there are some excellent books on pet psychology and behavior, such as *When Good Dogs Do Bad Things* by Siegal and Margolis, *Owner's Guide to Better Behavior in Dogs and Cats,* by William Campbell, and *Understanding Your Cat,* by Dr. Michael Fox, that will help you out further here.

Amazingly enough, a lot of "accidents" aren't accidents at all but failure of the master to provide his pet with even the most elementary training. Dogs and cats have a natural instinct to not foul their surroundings, and with a little encouragement they can be taught to be quite tidy in their elimination habits. With proper training, a good diet, and regular health care, your pet's nature calls shouldn't be an on-going problem for you.

But even the best pet is going to have an accident once in a while, so how do we handle them when they come along?

First of all, don't believe the claims you see or hear about miracle products that just "spray away" pet stains and odor. It just ain't so. There are hundreds of pet stain removers on the market, and none of them work without some effort. If the label says, "Just open the bottle and the chemical does the rest," be suspicious. And bear in mind that no one product can really deal effectively with both stain *and* odor. They're two separate problems—and odor is usually harder to get rid of than stain.

Also to be taken with a grain of salt are the "helpful hints" solutions such as vinegar and water, seltzer water, etc. While some of them work to a degree, none of these preparations are nearly as effective as the products manufactured specifically to deal with pet stains and odors.

Cleaning Up Urine

Urine is not a simple substance. It's composed of water, proteins, urea, uric acid, amino acids, ammonia, salts, and other inorganic compounds. When fresh, urine is almost always acidic, but it becomes alkaline as it ages. Urine is capable of staining a great many surfaces, is very hard to remove from fabrics once it dries, and has an offensive odor as well, which only gets worse with time.

If caught while fresh, a urine deposit is fairly easy to remove, and staining can often be prevented. If you catch the spot after it's been there awhile, but is still wet, urine can still be dealt with very successfully. But if urine isn't cleaned up within twenty-four to forty-eight hours, it will become very difficult, if not impossible, to remove. The salts and inorganic compounds that remain are not easily dissolved in water, and the acids produced as the urine decomposes often leave a permanent stain.

CLEANING URINE FROM HARD SURFACES

On a surface that doesn't absorb liquid, such as semigloss or gloss enamel paint, seamless vinyl flooring, or sealed concrete, urine wipes right up with no damage at all. (This should give you a few clues as to the interior decoration of your pet's living quarters.) Just blot the liquid up with paper towels, then clean the surface with a detergent solution. A squirt of common dish detergent in water will kill at least 90 percent of the bacteria in fresh urine, and should leave no appreciable odor.

Some surfaces, though "hard," are porous, and will absorb some of the urine. These include flat or matte-finish latex paint, unsealed concrete, and unfinished wood. Vinyl tile can also absorb liquids in the joints between the tiles. In cases like this, where some of the urine has actually been absorbed into the surface, odor can cling and stay, and a chemical deodorizer/cleaner should definitely be used. If the odor problem is serious, you'll want to seal (varnish or polyurethane or repaint) the surface after deodorizing to help seal in any residual odor so your pet can't smell it.

If you're cleaning up after a puppy in the process of being housebroken or an animal who's been breaking housetraining, be sure to spray the spot after you clean it with a chemical deodorizer, to discourage him from smelling the spot and using it again. The importance of getting rid of *all* the odor from a pet accident can't be overemphasized. It's been estimated that an animal's sense of smell is a hundred thousand times stronger than ours, and if there's one molecule of urine left our pets will smell it. And it'll signal them to a repeat performance in that spot. This is also why you should *never* attempt to clean a urine stain with ammonia or a cleaner containing ammonia. Ammonia gives off urinelike scent signals that will insure another pet mess in the very same spot.

CLEANING URINE OUT OF CARPETING

This is the biggie—the real challenge to pet owner and professional carpet cleaner alike. Urine spots in the carpet tend to soak down through the carpet and into the carpet backing and pad and even the subfloor beneath, making them very difficult to remove. The quicker you catch a urine stain, the better!

For a fresh urine stain on carpet, gently blot up all you can with paper towels, being careful not to spread the stain or to drive the remaining liquid deeper in-

to the carpet. (If your carpeting is treated with a soil retardant, it'll keep liquid spills of all kinds from soaking into the fiber, giving you time to blot them up.) After blotting up all the free liquid, put a clean terry towel or other absorbent material on the spot and apply pressure with your heel to absorb all the remaining liquid. Turn the towel over and press several times until you're not getting any more urine out. After blotting, use a chemical deodorizer/cleaner such as Nilotex or Dog-Tex, following the directions on the label. To be really safe, use a bacteria/enzyme digester. A chemical product may do the job if you catch the stain immediately, but a bacteria/enzyme digester is really the only way to completely eliminate the organic material down deep in the carpet that causes the odor from a pet stain in carpeting, especially one that's had a chance to penetrate.

To reach the urine down in the carpet fibers and backing, you have to get the deodorizing chemical or bacteria/enzyme solution down as far as the urine went. Apply to the carpet about $1\frac{1}{2}$ times as much solution as you estimate there was urine, and then work it into the carpet with your shoe or fingers. (It's a good idea to wear rubber gloves when you work on pet stains with your hands.) If it's a big spot or large area, don't try to spray or squirt it on—remove the cap and pour it on.

Then just step on the spot with your shoe and work the solution clear through the back of the carpet and into the pad until it feels squishy underfoot. If you're using a chemical deodorizer, after working the chemical in well, and letting it stay there for as long as the label recommends, use a clean towel to blot as much of the deodorizer as you can, using a towel under your foot and turning it until it comes up dry. If you're using a bacteria/enzyme product, leave the solution in the carpet for six or eight hours before you blot, so it can do its work. In dry climates, you may have to cover the spot with a piece of plastic wrap or a damp towel to keep it from drying out too soon (the beneficial bacteria will die if the spot dries up).

In dealing with any carpet stain, remember to always *blot,* not *scrub.* Scrubbing can damage the carpet fibers and may also spread the stain.

After you've blotted out as much as you can, put a dry towel over the stain and weigh it down with something heavy, like a brick or a couple of books, and it'll continue to absorb moisture for several hours. Then remove the towel and fluff up the carpet fibers to let the carpet finish drying.

If there's still a visible spot on the carpet after it dries, follow up with a water rinse or a carpet stain remover. Repeat the deodorizer or bacteria/enzyme solution if the odor isn't all gone.

Setting a lamp, chair, or large potted plant on a "repeat spot" after cleaning and deodorizing may help discourage encores, or you may want to follow up the above procedures with an application of a stain repellent such as Pet Proof for extra protection.

URINE STAINS ON CLOTHING AND WASHABLE FABRICS

Pretreat the stain with a liquid enzyme detergent according to directions, and then launder the item with chlorine bleach, if it's safe for the fabric—otherwise use a color-safe oxygen bleach such as Biz or Clorox 2. An alternative method is to soak the garment in water and ammonia solution ($\frac{1}{4}$ cup of ammonia to $\frac{1}{2}$ gallon water) if the fabric can handle it (don't use ammonia on wool or silk) then apply a chemical deodorizer. If you use a bacteria/enzyme digester, limit the prerinse to water only. And don't dry the article in the dryer till you're sure the stain is gone, because heat will set stains.

For urine stains in upholstery, remove foam cushions from their fabric covers if possible, then treat the covers just like clothing. If the covering isn't removable, treat overstuffed furniture just as you would carpeting. To be sure the treatment is effective, you'll have to soak the cushions with chemical deodorizer or bacteria/enzyme solution just as deep as the urine went. Be cautioned, though, that some of the stuffing materials used in upholstered furniture may stain the cover fabric when the upholstery is as thoroughly wet as this.

For urine stains on drapes or curtains, apply a pet spot and stain remover such as Nilotex. Or take the drapes to a dry cleaner, and be sure to explain what and where the stains are.

Old or Widespread Urine Stains in Carpeting

Even when old and dry, a urine stain will have a strong odor, which becomes even more pronounced in wet weather or high humidity. Many a professional cleaner has learned this to his dismay, trying to restore a urine-stained carpet. As soon as he puts a little water on the rug, the dormant or "residual" odor roars to life, and the horrified owner cries: "What have you done to my carpet? You're supposed to clean it, and you've made it smell worse than ever!"

Cleaning professionals use a tool called a moisture probe to locate dampness and water damage on floor cleanup jobs. Even if the carpet doesn't feel wet, these probes sense the salts left behind

by drying urine and will identify every place the animal has wet. They can even find ancient dried urine spots such as those left behind by the pet a previous tenant may have had. Probes are battery-powered and give off a beep when they locate an accident site—the bigger the spot, the louder and faster the beeps. Moisture probes such as the Outright Urine Detector Probe only cost about a hundred dollars and might be a worthwhile investment to save a $3,000 carpet.

Your best chance against an old urine stain is a bacteria/enzyme digester. But bear in mind, when you're using it, that the bacteria will release ammonia from the urine as they digest it. If the spot you're dealing with is a multiple accident site, the bacteria may produce so much ammonia that an alkaline atmosphere is created, which will interfere with, or stop, the bacteria's action. So, in cases like this, you need to neutralize the spot after four to six hours with a solution of one cup white vinegar to a gallon of warm water. Rinse the area with this solution and then apply a fresh batch of bacteria/enzyme solution. An alternate approach in such cases is to rinse the area with plain water to reduce the urine concentration before applying the digester.

WORST CASE SCENARIO
If urine damage is extensive and has occurred over a long period of time, it's virtually impossible to eliminate every trace of stain and odor. If you have a carpet in this condition, consider calling in a professional deodorizing technician for an opinion. This isn't just any old cleaning contractor or carpet cleaner, but a professional cleaner well experienced and trained in the specific techniques of urine stain removal. If the situation is really bad, he'll probably rec-

ommend replacing the carpet and pad, and sealing the subfloor underneath. If he feels that the carpeting can be saved, it'll involve a process something along these lines: Thoroughly clean the carpet with hot water and a strong extraction "steam" cleaner. Lift the carpet in the affected area and remove the pad underneath; possibly replace the tack strip if it's badly affected. Clean and disinfect the subfloor, and possibly seal it with a pigmented shellac or lacquer sealer. Install a new carpet pad, possibly one that has a polyethylene vapor barrier. Apply a chemical deodorizer/cleaner or a bacteria/enzyme digester to the carpet back, and pull it through to the face yarns with the extractor. Dry and reinstall the carpet. Thoroughly clean the whole room.

Even after all of this, permanent stains may remain. Sometimes these will respond to bleaching and/or dyeing, but with drastic measures like these, the cure can be worse than the disease. Therefore, you should consider them only as a last resort, after you've tried everything else.

If you have a proposal from a deodorizing firm to restore badly urine-damaged carpet that leaves out any of these steps, the work may not completely eliminate the odor problem.

Obviously, this is a time-consuming and expensive process, and one that would be ill-advised if the value of the carpeting involved doesn't justify it. In most cases, replacement is the most realistic solution to widespread urine damage. The key, of course, is to avoid letting things get to this point. If you make sure your pet is thoroughly housebroken, catch and clean up any accidents as soon as they occur, and seek out and cure the cause of any persistent behavior problems that occur, you can avoid permanent damage to your home and furnishings.

Cleaning Up Feces

When the dog or cat poops on the floor, it isn't the potential disaster a urine stain can be. On carpet, you can simply pick up reasonably dry, compact feces with your hand slipped inside a plastic bag, or with a dustpan or two pieces of cardboard. Then treat the carpet with the pet stain product of your choice.

Since this type of soil is almost always confined to the surface of the carpet, a chemical deodorizer/cleaner should do the job here. Be sure to remove all the solid waste you can before applying any cleaner or deodorizer—it's a deodorizer, not a miracle worker. An aged, dried-up #2 deposit may have to be soaked and scrubbed gently to get rid of any remaining residue after you've removed the loose material from the surface.

If your pet has diarrhea, or if the stool is combined with urine, the liquids may have soaked down into the carpet, and you'll have to use the more involved procedure described for urine removal. Where you have a stool with considerable liquid content that's soaked into the carpet, use a bacteria/enzyme digester. Any other cleaning method is going to leave some organic matter imbedded in the recesses of the carpet and pad.

Pet foods with heavy dyes (to make the food look nice and meaty—to us, not our pet) will stain carpeting and other home surfaces if your pet has an accident after eating such food. The red dyes are always the worst on carpets. Dyes in pet food also make it hard to use the stools as an indicator of your pet's general health, and many dyes are also potential cancer risks. Dye content will be listed on the package, so you should be able to bypass the rations if you're so inclined. (Pinkish stains from pet food dyes on a light-colored carpet may respond to bleaching, but this is a job you should refer to a professional carpet cleaner.)

ON HARD SURFACES

like vinyl flooring, #2 cleanup is a simple process no matter how much liquid is involved. Simply blot or pick up the liquid and solid waste and then clean and deodorize in one step with a chemical deodorizer/cleaner. On a hard floor that's been sealed or waxed, simply wiping with a solution of water and dish detergent is usually good enough.

Vomit Cleanup

Dogs and cats have occasional bouts of vomiting, just as we do, for a variety of reasons. Cats seem more prone to vomit than dogs, and the cause can be anything from hairballs in the stomach to overeating to a serious illness. If you find your dog or cat vomiting but they don't show any other signs of illness (fever, diarrhea, sluggishness, blood in the vomit or stool), you may not have to rush him off to the vet. Often you can pinpoint the cause of the problem when

you think about it—motion sickness from traveling, eating grass, eating rodents, overeating, a change in diet, or too much fat in the diet.

If you're not sure what caused it, but the animal seems otherwise healthy, try withholding food and water for twenty-four hours, and the condition will probably take care of itself. If the pet continues to have dry heaves after being off food and water for a time, or if you find blood or worms in the expelled material, you should consult your vet as soon as possible. Often, though, a pet will just get an upset stomach for one reason or another, then he'll throw up and feel fine.

But no matter what the cause, cleaning up upchuck isn't fun. In addition to being smelly and unsightly, vomit contains gastric juices from the stomach, which are strong acids. These will bleach the color out of many fabrics very quickly, so the first thing to do is to remove as much of the liquid and solid material as possible. Scrape it up with a squeegee and dustpan or a couple of pieces of cardboard, or use an absorbent compound.

Sprinkle the absorbent (usually composed of clay granules) onto the spot, leave it there for a few minutes, then scoop it back up. The absorbent will absorb the liquid and solidify the mess so it's easier to remove—you can even sweep it up. Absorbents (Big D Granular Deodorant is the name of one good one) usually contain a deodorizer and a pleasant-smelling masking fragrance as well, so all in all they make the job of vomit cleanup quite a bit more bearable.

As soon as you get up all the loose material you can, flood the spot with water to dilute the remaining gastric acids and prevent bleaching of your carpet, flooring, or upholstery. I recom-

mend you use a bacteria/enzyme digester on the stain, so limit the first rinse to
water only. As with urine staining,
you'll have to clean the carpet with a
spot and stain remover after using a
bacteria/enzyme digester, to remove
any remaining discoloration.

If you plan to use a chemical deodor-
izer/cleaner on the stain, rinse the area
first with ¼ cup of household ammonia
in ½ gallon of warm water. The ammonia, being alkaline, will quickly neutralize the acids in the vomit and help
prevent staining. (But don't use ammonia on wool or silk—it can be damag-
ing.)

The problem of red dyes in pet food is
more serious here because vomit is
more liquid, and its gastric acids make
it more likely that the dye will affect the
carpet fibers. The best solution to this
problem is simply to avoid feeding your
pets food that contains red dye.

If a pet has vomited on clothing, treat
it as you would a urine stain on clothing
(see page 65), after you scrape off all you
can.

When it comes to accidents, remember that prevention is the first line of defense. Make sure your pet is trained to
meet your expectations. Get advice
from your vet on proper diet and regular
health care. Also be aware that your pet
will occasionally have a problem and be
prepared to deal with it. Have the necessary cleaning aids and odor neutralizers
on hand to deal effectively with accidents and stains, act quickly, and you
can avoid permanent damage to your
home and furnishings.

Some Pointers for Accident Patrol

Be sure to remove the source first:
Whether you're trying to deal with a
fresh urine stain or a #2 deposit
that's been hidden under the couch
for months, do be sure to remove
the *source* of the odor as far as
practical, before dousing the area
with chemicals and cleaning or
deodorizing solutions. (This same
rule applies to cleaning the pet
feeding or food storage area, pet
bedding, etc.)

Be ready ahead: Since swift action
is essential, you'll need to have your
supplies on hand ahead of time to be
prepared to fend off pet stains and
odors. The chemical deodorizer/
cleaners and the bacteria/enzyme
digesters are the most useful and
effective for the tough jobs involved
in pet stain and odor removal. So
buy them and put them away with
your other cleaning equipment, so
you'll be ready when the time comes.
Stockpile a few clean terrycloth
towels or cleaning cloths with your
supplies, too.

A handy way to use and apply
bacteria/enzyme solution is in a
plastic spray bottle. In the case of
the Outright bacteria/enzyme
product, you can avoid mixing up
more of the (perishable) solution
than you need by filling one bottle
with water and one with the bacteria/
enzyme concentrate. Then, since an
Outright bacteria/enzyme solution is
always diluted 2:1, you can just give
the spot one squirt of concentrate
followed by two squirts of water.

CHAPTER 5

Hairy Animal Tales

Stroking an animal's soft pelt is an entirely pleasant sensation, as long as the hair is still attached to the animal. Once it's flying loose you can stroke it with every cleaning tool imaginable and only end up exasperated. Cleaning up animal hair is one of the acid tests of pet patience.

Pets don't merely leave hair lying around, they deposit it over and under every piece of furniture and fixture and room in the home, and they manage to get us moving targets, too. The hair problem is worse than a few loose strands floating around. Fur, hair, and dander (the tiny particles of dead skin that every animal sheds) can cause and aggravate allergies, contribute to indoor pollution, give cats indigestion (from hairballs), irritate guests (when it sticks to their clothes), as well as keep the pet cleaner in perpetual motion.

Shedding used to be a once or maybe twice a year problem, as our pets shed their heavy winter coats in the springtime and grew it back in the fall. They needed a heavier coat to protect them from winter cold, and sensibly got rid of it before the heat of summer. They begin to shed when given the signal to do so by warmer weather and longer daylight hours, but our modern indoor lighting, heating, and air conditioning throw the process off and often cause pets to shed constantly.

If you feel your pet is shedding excessively, it might be caused by a too-tight collar or by stress, such as from being boarded or hospitalized.

I learned that *diet* can affect a pet's coat back when I was ten years old, working on our farm. Our black Lab began to look sleek and shiny, and my father said, "That dog looks *too* good—he's been sucking eggs." Sure enough, we began to find empty eggs with a hole punched in them. That egg diet sure slicked Rover up!

Your pet might be shedding excessively simply because he doesn't have enough fatty acid in his diet. To remedy this, there are products made just for the purpose, such as Linatone, by Lambert Kay and F.A. granules or liquid by Beecham.

Grooming to Control Shedding

By grooming I don't mean cutely coiffured haircuts or colorful claw polish, but simply removing the loose hair from your pet before it lands on your furnishings.

We too often think that grooming is only for poodles and Persians, and that

ol' Fang, macho creature that he is, would never need or allow such a sissy thing to be done to him. But every cat and dog needs regular vigorous brushing and gentle combing, and the longhaired ones will develop real problems if they're not groomed regularly. Longhaired cats pick up a lot of fur on their tongues as they groom themselves. They swallow the hairs, which form into indigestible wads or strings in their stomachs and intestines. These wads can cause vomiting (although vomiting may not get the wad up), and even death.

Grooming will make your pet's coat shinier and his skin healthier, and keep him smelling pleasant. Grooming also gives you the opportunity to check your pet for parasites like ticks and fleas, and for cuts and injuries.

Start grooming your pet as a pup or kitten, or as soon as you get him. Gradually accustom him to your grooming and handling of every part of his body. Some pets will even allow you to use a vacuum on them to remove the loose fur (and fleas and flea eggs), if you get them accustomed to it early.

Don't wait to groom until your pet gets scroungy looking. Groom at least twice a week during shedding season, or if your pet has a very dense coat that's prone to matting.

You'll need some tools to groom properly. Exactly what will depend on the breed of cat or dog you have, and its hair length and type.

- *For shorthaired and smooth-coated pets, use a soft bristle brush or a grooming glove. This is a mitt with short bristles on one side that slips right over your hand.*

- *For pets with medium-length soft or wiry coats, use a slicker brush, a rectangular-shaped flat-backed brush with short bent-wire teeth set in a rubber base. These come in different sizes and with "firm" or "fine" bristles.*

- *Use a pin brush on longhaired pets— an oval brush with rows of round tipped metal pins and a long handle.*

- *Combs work best on longhaired pets and pets with undercoats. In general, a comb will remove loose hair better than a brush.*

Secrets of Good Grooming

Brush or comb in the direction the hair grows. If your pet has a thick coat, be sure you're getting all the way down to the skin. If there's *lots* of loose hair in the coat, brush "against the grain" first, then finish up in the direction of the hair growth. Carefully cut out any mats that won't yield to combing. If you come across a burr or sticktight, crush it with pliers; then you should be able to comb the fragments out without too much trouble.

Use your plastic trigger-spray bottle for yet another pet purpose here, to apply antistatic coat conditioner or other liquid products, full-strength or diluted, as you groom.

The grooming area should be a quiet one and your pet shouldn't be distracted by other pets, children, or loud noises. If you can, use a firm surface such as the tabletop or the top of an automatic dryer; there are also special grooming tables widely available.

Especially for small and medium-size animals, a sturdy nonslip surface that brings your pet up to a height that makes it easy to reach every part of him without bending will make you much less likely to skip grooming sessions. Each time you brush or groom the pet use this same area.

To try the vacuum approach, get the quietest vacuum you can find and an extra-long hose; the longer the hose, the farther away all that pet-threatening noise will be. And get a grooming attachment—a round upholstery head with tiny rubber fingers instead of bristles. Vacuum up the dead hair as you brush it loose, and run the grooming head gently over the coat in the direction the hair grows, as well as against it. Many pets will actually enjoy the sensation, after they get used to the noise of the vacuum.

Talking to your pet through the whole process, and praising him as you go, will usually help him cooperate. As will stopping for a few moments or changing the grooming site or letting him shift position when he gets too uneasy. If he tries to get away, have someone steady him while you groom.

Wash your hands when you're finished and give the grooming table or area a quick cleaning with Chlorasan solution. Simply spray the surface with the solution and then wipe it off with a damp sponge or paper towel. Wash grooming tools in a mild detergent periodically, as you would a hairbrush.

Stepping up your dog's bathing schedule (such as to once a week during heavy shedding season) will also help head off hair. Bathing will loosen and remove dead hair before it's spread all over the house. If you do bathe a pet as often as this, it's extra-important to use a shampoo that's properly balanced for your pet. Give your pet a good vigorous body massage before you plop him into the tub, to loosen the fur that's about to fall out anyway. Longhaired dogs can sometimes send enough hair down the drain to clog the pipes. Make sure your drain has a good metal filtering screen so the hair won't go down the drain. (In extreme cases, consider trimming a heavy-coated dog's coat extra short to reduce shedding fallout. He won't look like he's supposed to according to the dog encyclopedia, but the shorter hair that drops afterward may be noticed less.)

10,000 Miracle Hair Pickup Tools

In teaching hundreds of cleaning seminars to audiences that include a lot of enthusiastic pet owners, I'm flooded with devices to try. Some of these do pick up a lot of hair at first, but then usually 50 percent less with each swipe. Fond as I am of them for other uses, squeegees don't really do an effective job on hair. And foam pickup devices are less effectual as they age—like by about the third time you use them.

The tape or tacky paper roller devices (that look like the old German hand grenades) do a pretty good job of pickup. They even pull embedded hair out of fabric. But they only work well as long as the adhesive is fresh—you have to keep peeling down to a fresh new layer. And while these may be among the best for a limited area like clothing, this can be an expensive way to clean a couch or sitting room. If you are going to use a tape roller on furniture and the like, there's at least one model (the Magic Pickup) that's built like a small paint roller, to make it easier to use on large flat surfaces.

Many people use masking tape for removing hair from furniture and clothes, but though it's more universally available, it's almost as expensive as the rollers for use on large areas and more awkward to handle—you waste all the tape that sticks to itself and sticks to you. If you're going to use tape, better yet is that wide plastic packing tape—it's wider and stickier. The red velour brushes do a fairly good job on short hairs, but they don't work on embedded hair. And they won't work well at all if you don't keep them cleaned off.

As for the old housecleaner's trick of rubbing a damp sponge or damp cloth over the surface to be de-haired, this technique is a useful one—as long as the damp cloth is stickier than the surface. If you use a damp cloth on baseboard, the hair *will* all come off and cling to the rag. But try the same thing on drapes, upholstered furniture, or carpet, and 75 percent of it will roll up into little wads and stay there. A damp cloth works on slick surfaces because the water cuts the static electricity that causes the hair to cling. You can also spray a hard surface lightly with water from your spray bottle and then wipe up the hair with a paper towel.

A woman in Eugene, Oregon, gave me the only hair pickup tool that's ever impressed me. This "pet rake" had crimped nylon bristles, and I promised to try it on the bed where Snoopy, our thirteen-year-old shameless shedder, spent most of his senior-citizen time. I couldn't believe it—it actually worked! I've bought and used lots of these since then, and everyone who tries them says the same thing. It gets hair (and for that matter thread and lint) up quicker and more quietly than a vacuum can. When you sweep it toward you with light strokes, it gets the hair up easily off upholstered furniture, cushions, draperies, stairs, car interiors, bedding, along the edge of the carpet, and under the bed. Use it on edge and it'll even get the hair out of tufting, cording, and seams. These are not easy to find in stores or catalogs, so I've added it to the pro supplies available to my readers by mail (see page 4).

Hair on the Floor

On soft flooring, vacuum it off. Easier said than done, you say? We've all been in the situation where we made sixteen passes with the vacuum over a clinging, contemptuous strand of hair which completely ignored us and refused to lift up off the floor. Why, we wonder, can that vacuum manage to pick up paper clips, nails, BB's, coins, and even rocks, yet leave feather-light hair lying on the floor, making a fool of us?

The steel balls sucked up so impressively at vacuum demonstrations are just slightly smaller than the vacuum hose. Once in the hose, it's like blowing a dart through a blow gun—there's no way for the air to go around the ball, it has to push (or pull) it along the tube. A hair or thread on the carpet, on the other hand, is hard to dislodge with suction alone. The air current can't get ahold of it so it just flows fiercely over the surface of the hair, never getting behind it to push it loose.

The vacuum's beater bar is what gives us an even chance with clinging hair. It can root out embedded fur and pull it in. Lots of vacuums have beater bars, but they're often not adjusted low enough to be able to reach and grab all the hair and other fine debris. Vacuums have low to high pile settings that determine how low the beater bar will reach—so be sure to read your vacuum's instruction booklet and adjust it accordingly.

The brushes on the beater bar are often worn down and no longer effective. Check out your beater bar's brushes, and replace them if necessary. Likewise, the belt that turns the beater bar may be stretched or cracked or otherwise worn so that it slips, or doesn't turn the beater bar fast enough. Check the belt regularly and replace it when necessary with a new, tight belt.

A professional dust mop is the fastest, easiest, and most effective way to collect and remove pet hair from every type of hard surface. Most supermarket or discount-store dust mops are just dust distributors; what you want is a 12- or 18-inch professional swivel-head mop from a janitorial supply store. Here are the pro secrets of technique.

1. Trim: *Your dust mop may have strings around the edges that are a little too long, so they end up scattering hair up on the baseboards. Take a pair of scissors and trim about ½ inch off the strands all around the outside of the mop. This will make the mop less floppy and enable you to control the dust and hair better.*

2. Treat: *Dust mops are most effective when they've been sprayed with dust mop treatment. You can get professional dust mop treatment at the janitorial supply store, or just use a little furniture polish or Endust. Spray the head of the mop generously and let it stand so the oil can distribute itself evenly through the yarn; you might even want to leave the mop overnight before you use it. Now the mop will get a magnetic hold on that hair.*

3. Use: *Push the mop in one long continual stroke in front of you and keep it in constant contact with the floor. Once you start, don't pick the mop up and always keep the same side headed forward—if you lift or reverse the mop head you'll lose some of the dirt. With a swivel-head mop you don't have to lift to get into corners or under and around things—you just swivel the head. Mop the area closest to the baseboard last.*

4. Clean: *A dust mop will collect and hold most of the hair and other loose debris it picks up on the edges and*

bottom of the mop. To get rid of this stuff, shake the mop outside, or inside a large plastic bag. When the head gets dirty, shake it well and throw it in the washer all by itself. Wash in hot water with a good grease-cutting detergent and maybe a little bleach, then tumble it dry like a towel. Don't hang it out to dry or it'll be stiff—it needs to fluff up in the dryer.

5. Store *a dust mop head up and away from the wall. A janitor's closet hook (from a janitorial supply or home improvement store) will keep the mop a little distance from the wall, or you can just slip a sturdy plastic bag over the mop head when it's in storage to keep oily stains off the wall.*

Getting Hair Off Furniture

Vacuuming doesn't always remove hair, especially if you use a canister vacuum attachment without a beater bar, which is what we often use on furniture. You need an attachment with stiff bristles to *loosen* the hair so it can be removed. A stiff brush head will get hair off almost everything, from velvet to flocked wallpaper.

You can and should vacuum sturdy upholstered seats using the vacuum's beater bar, just as you do the carpet. If you do this regularly hair won't have a chance to accumulate. Delicate fabrics and loose weaves, however, should *not* be vacuumed in this way. On a limited area like furniture or drapes, you can use a tape roller or masking tape or a velour brush.

As for the hair that ends up in places like baseboards, the kickboard underneath the kitchen cabinets, and other places under and beneath that the broom or vacuum always miss, a damp cloth or paper towel will take it right up.

hair-laden fabric, nor will dry cleaning. Hair comes off cotton and polyester fairly well in a washer, but sticks tight to a napped or fuzzy material like flannel or wool. Slick or smooth fabric surfaces repel hair, or at least enable it to be removed more easily.

Professional launderers say "We do the same thing you do, we pick it off with our fingers or roll masking tape around our hand and lift it off." Dry cleaners do the same thing. There's no magic cure, but there are a few things that will help.

Shake the article outside, if possible, before you launder it. Take large items such as blankets down to the Laundromat and use one of the large-capacity washers, the ones with the bigger and stronger drums. Then wash the article, making sure there's plenty of water swishing around with it to rinse away the hair. Use your regular detergent and then add a little Chlorasan to the rinse water for an extra attack on germs and odor. If possible, give the clothes an extra rinse cycle to help float the hair off. Take the article out when it's done and shake it while it's still damp. Then put it in the dryer with three or four fabric softener sheets—this will reduce the static electricity that holds the hair to the fabric. You can also use liquid fabric softener, either in the wash or rinse cycle. Putting an article in a dryer set on cool is another way to help remove animal (or human) hair. Then shake the article again when it comes out of the dryer. Whatever hair is left now will have to be taken off with tape.

Afterwards, wipe out the washer and dryer—especially the dryer—with a damp cloth to remove loose hair. Empty the lint filter of both dryer and washer promptly.

A disposable cloth is really best because it's hard to rinse or wash hair out of a cloth—you often end up just spreading it around onto other surfaces.

Hair on Clothes and Blankets

The washing process alone won't necessarily get all the hair off a heavily

A Good Bed...
Will Lessen Pet
Mess

If the pet home base—the bed—is appealing and comfortable your pet will spend a lot of his sleeping, rolling, and shedding time there instead of on your furniture and carpeting.

Most cats and dogs, as their fatal attraction to human furniture has proven over the years, do prefer "soft" spots (except for the very hairy northern breeds who may actually prefer a cool hard surface). A padded bed is especially important for older dogs and large heavy breeds, to prevent sores and calluses. Small dogs and cats often prefer to have the ultra-snug atmosphere of an enclosed or high-sided bed. In general, cats are cubbyholers, dogs are nesters.

Cats can be very individualistic and hard to figure, and they actually prefer a bed above ground level—especially if there are children or other pets in the house. For this reason the cat perch (usually a wooden or carpeted shelf that can be attached to the windowsill) might please your pet. Sunsill is one popular brand.

The best pet bed is the simplest. It doesn't need carved legs or elaborate headboards for your pet to chew up and scatter all over the house. Two of the simplest pet beds are the soft padded cushions with sturdy fabric covers and the simple, plastic platform raised slightly off the floor.

No matter how nice it looks, smells, and feels, make sure the bed is washable—preferably machine washable and dryable. Does the bed itself—or the cushion in it—have a washable cover that can be removed like a slipcover? Or if it has no cushion or cover, can the material of the bed itself be cleaned easily? You also want a surface that will hold up to scratching, abrasion and wear. Good choices here include polycotton, polycotton twill or polycotton poplin, cotton duck, denim, tight-weave muslin, even oxford cloth or 100 percent medium-weight cotton.

The Doskocil Company of Arlington, Texas, makes attractive beds for both cats and dogs that are exceptionally easy to clean and sanitize because they're one-piece molded polyethylene. They come with a fluffy washable mat that fits inside.

If your pet bed has a wooden or wicker base or enclosure, be sure it's sealed with varnish or polyurethane to make it waterproof and washable. And be sure to buy (or make) an extra cover for your pet's bed so he won't be hovering around homeless on washday.

You *want* the surface of the pet bed to absorb pet body oils and secretions and spills, so this is one place you don't want to use stain repellent. But you don't want the filling to be absorbent, so polystyrene beads are a good choice for a soft insulated bed. Cedar shavings are much favored as a pet bedding because they're believed to repel fleas and other insects. But it's never been actually proven, and bird dog fanciers insist that constant exposure to cedar and its pungent odor blunts a pet's delicate scenter. Pine wood shavings with a little flea powder added might do just as well, or even better. Foam rubber is *not* recommended, as it absorbs odor and poses a safety hazard if a dog chews through to it.

The Weekly Once-Over

Once a week, shake out the bed and vacuum off the padding. Wipe down any hard surfaces and the floor around and under the bed with a deodorizing cleaner or an all-purpose cleaning solution. To disinfect these areas from time to time, spray or wipe them with a Chlorasan solution, then rinse well. Once in a while take up grimy toys (if they're washable) and soak them in Chlorasan solution, scrub them off, then rinse.

Wash the cover of your pet's bed every two weeks or so. Use a lint roller on it first to remove most of the loose hair, then wash it separately in hot water and detergent, with a capful of deodorizing cleaner added. If you want to disinfect, soak in a Chlorasan solution before washing.

Location

Dogs, especially, like to be in a position to hear and see household activities, so their bed ought to be somewhere right off the main living area of the house. Pick a place that isn't smack in the middle of the traffic patterns, and never put the dog bed or box on or near steps. The room you're likely to confine your pet in while you're away is a good place for the pet bed.

Most animals can take cold a lot better than they can take drafts. Never put a bed in a drafty area, or very close to a door. Concrete holds heat and cold—seemingly forever. Eighty percent of the time it's cold, and a thin towel or rag on the floor in the garage or in the dog run isn't very considerate of you. A 3/4-inch thick sheet of sealed plywood (with a couple of narrow strips of wood nailed to the underside to keep it off the ground) under the towel or blanket will keep the concrete from passing its cold into your pet's body—prolonging your pet's life as well as keeping it sleeping where you want it to.

For outdoor pet beds in the doghouse, shed, garage, barn, or dog run, it's even more important to have a dry undrafty spot that's also elevated a few inches above the ground to prevent chill transfer. The "sleeping compartment" should be small enough to help hold in the dog's body heat.

Outdoors, the bedding can be shredded newspapers or clean dry straw (hay

is dusty and may contain weeds to which your pet is allergic). Wood shavings—from a pet supplier, not a sawmill—are even better.

Pets Lying on Furniture

One of the great battles of the pet household between *them* (the pets) and *us* (the alleged masters)—and often also between the various human members of the household—is our pets' endless efforts to occupy the furniture.

If you don't want your pet on the furniture, you have to teach him that it's absolutely OUT! The hard part about this is managing to be consistent. You have to teach him this right from the start, from the time he's a pup. He must understand that it's *never* okay to sit on the furniture—or that it's only okay when we specifically tell him so with a certain command. Our pets suffer a lot, when it comes to furniture lying, from our own vacillation over the question of whether they're allowed there or not.

If he's an adult animal and has already entrenched his position, rigorous retraining is in order. Give him a whack on the rump with your hand or a fly swatter, lift or push him off, or squirt him with your Scat bottle—all the while uttering a loud and firm *"no"* or *"off"* or *"down."*

No matter what method you use, you have to stick with it and evict him every time you catch him. Then encourage him to go to *his* bed and praise and reward him when he does.

Make sure your pet has its own soft and inviting place to lie down and nap and snooze—a nice comfy pet bed. Reinforce that it's *his* bed by making the whole area around the bed clearly his area—an appealing, warm, undrafty place with some toys and maybe a pet mat. Teach him the word "place" or "bed" and train him to understand that *here* is where he goes when he wants to rest, sleep, or just watch the passing parade.

If your pet stays off the furniture while you're there, but you keep coming home to a warm couch, you have to get more devious.

The following are among the arsenal of off-putters you can employ:

- *Cover the furniture in jeopardy with an old sheet or bedspread to protect it while you're gone, and take it off when you return (the resignation approach).*

- *Booby trap the furniture with mousetraps, four or five on a couch, say, covered with newspapers and taped down, balloons taped to the furniture, or shake cans. If you've already trained your pet to detest shake cans on sight, one such can perched in solitary magnificence on your prize sofa might be enough to do it.*

- *Apply one of the aerosol pet repellents made for inside use to a rag or towel and drape it over the furniture you want to protect.*

- *Make the furniture repulsive by cat or dog standards by covering the seat with aluminum foil, or the whole thing with plastic sheeting. (Dogs and cats dislike the feel and sound of foil, and cats hate to lie on plastic.)*

- *Confine him—use a closed door or crate or pet gate to keep him out of the prime-furnishings patch.*

If, on the other hand, you feel that your pet is entitled to be up on the furniture, make sure all your upholstered furniture is treated with a stain repellent such as Scotchgard. Or you could designate one piece of furniture—a "sacrificial chair," say—that your pet is allowed on. Cover it with a big heavy old quilt or an easily washable spread, or make a terry cloth cover for the cushion your pet favors. Wash the spread or cover regularly.

And of course, choose new furnishings accordingly. Rugged fabrics that resist staining and scratching and don't hold hair are the best bet.

Strange Bedfellows

Pets on the bed mean loose hair on and in the bed, stains, and all the other cleaning complications of pets on the furniture. Plus some extra problems: ringworm, ticks, mites, and diseases that our pets may harbor, especially if they're outside animals. Mattresses and beds make excellent homesites for the fleas only too likely to infest our pets. And for those of us allergic to cats or dogs, the bed is the worst possible place we can allow a pet to be.

A pup or kitten or very small dog could also be injured by our midnight rolls and tosses—or they could fall off the bed and get hurt. Cats, being nocturnal animals by nature, have to re-adapt their schedule to sleep with us. And dogs can be so encouraged by the thought that they get to sleep in this obvious power location—the bed—that they may decide it's their bed, that *they're* top dog and in control, and can even become dangerously aggressive.

You can train your pet to stay off the bed, if he's already encroached on it, by any of the training methods described earlier. Give your pet a sense of togetherness and security—without being right up there under the covers with you—by putting his bed in the same room with yours (unless you're allergic to him).

If you do decide to allow your pet on the bed make sure it has an easily washable spread that camouflages your pet's hair. A printed spread will serve this purpose better than a plain solid color. See that your pet stays on top of this spread—not under the covers or on the pillows. You'll also want to wash the blankets more often (a little Chlorasan added to the rinse water wouldn't hurt). If your pet sleeps with you, it's extra important that you brush him often—even daily.

Make sure your pet is healthy—disease and parasite-free—before letting him sleep with you. This means a checkup every six months or so to catch pet health problems before they become your health problems.

Bath Time

Kathy Walter was a student of mine at a college professional cleaning course, and the letter she wrote me could sum it all up.

Dear Don,

My husband was out of town for a few days and I decided to surprise him when he returned with a nice clean dog. With the help of my son, I got the dog in the tub and proceeded to lather up "Sam." He was quite taken with the lather and began licking it off. I figured this was fine because at least he stood still and was easy to wash. But he soon tired of the soap bubbles and bounded out of the tub, headed for the back door. Sprinting after him, I slipped on the wet floor, twisting my ankle and hitting my elbow. The dog, of course, had stopped long enough in several spots to shake himself vigorously and dirty suds ran down half the walls in the house.

After a lively race in the backyard and a quick roll in the freshly plowed garden, we had the dog back in the house. Naturally, he stopped in the living room to roll his newly acquired mud all over the carpet. We resumed the bath, and within minutes Sam started to gag. (I guess the lather he ate, along with the rousting race in the yard, made him sick to his stomach.) Again he leaped out of the tub and before we could recapture him, he vomited several times in the dining room. We caught him again, cleaned up the mess, and went back to the bath.

The next day the house smelled like a thousand-pound wet dog. All the dog hair we'd washed down the drain had collected in the trap. I called a plumber to clean the trap, and now the drain smelled better, but the carpet was dirty and stank. As if in answer to my prayers, a vacuum cleaner salesman appeared at the door and offered to clean my carpet if I would listen to a sales presentation. So my carpet was cleaned, though I had to sit through a two-hour sales pitch that left me late getting the kids from school, late starting dinner, and totally unprepared for the ten Cub Scouts I'd promised an afternoon of leathercraft.

The next morning Sam had sore paws and began scratching his ear, and as we learned at the vet's, the ear had water in it from the fateful bath. And Sam's sore paws and rear were the result of being on the freshly cleaned carpet before it had dried. We left with ointments for both ends of the dog and all four feet.

Now all of us expert pet bathers reading Kathy's story sigh and say "Well, no wonder—she did everything wrong," but we know in our hearts that no bathing of pets is without some mess and strain. You could think of pet bathing as making an angel food cake—after hours of work you end up with a fantastic fluffy final result that makes all the mess and effort worth it!

Pets do have to be bathed from time to time, but not as often as we might think. We moderns are bath and shower crazy. Not long ago, a weekly bath was acceptable; now everyone is in the shower for an hour, even twice daily. So we tend to think our pets need a frequent bath or washing too—but not so! Your special pet or situation may be different than the average, but all the experts agree: If a pet is groomed as often as he should be—several times a week, at least—he'll rarely need a bath.

There are healthy, happy, attractive show-quality dogs that have never had a bath—ever! For a hairy creature like a pet, brushing does as good or better a job of removing dirt, dander, excess oil, and even fleas than the immerse-in-water-and-scrub ritual. In general, a dog should be bathed only if he looks dirty, smells bad, or gets into something awful. Or after he swims in polluted, chlorine-treated, or salt water. There are also some breeds like Airedales and Scotties whose hair holds dirt that can't easily be removed by brushing.

Outdoor dogs should definitely be bathed *less* often because the natural oils in their coats, which bathing removes, help protect them from the weather. If your dog has a BO problem or you're allergic to pet dander, you may want to wash him once a month or so, but the most you should ever wash a dog for any reason is once a week.

If you bathe your pet too often his skin and fur will dry out. And wet animals are extra susceptible to drafts and chills, so pups under three months should never be bathed, and very old dogs and pups under six months, only when absolutely necessary. Very young and old animals don't have the resistance to fight the respiratory infections, etc., that might follow. You also never want to bathe a sick pet or one near the end of pregnancy.

The same general rules of when to bathe apply to cats, just add the words: "or even less often." Neutered cats, especially, tend to have less body odor than dogs, and cats groom themselves more often. And cats make dogs' attitude toward bathing look positively enthusiastic. But longhaired cats, especially, sometimes get into something that really needs to be washed off, or they may need a flea shampoo or a bath for other medicinal reasons.

You might get by with a waterless bath or no-rinse shampoo. To clean a pup, an older dog, or a cat, especially, without wetting them, use a dry shampoo to remove the dirt and excess oil in the coat. Several powders and spray foams are commercially produced for just this purpose, or you can use ordinary cornstarch. Simply sprinkle or spray it on, work it into the coat well, leave it on for a a few minutes, and then brush your pet vigorously until you get it all back out. This process is best performed outside, if possible, for obvious reasons. (You can also use a no-rinse shampoo, which is applied directly from the bottle, worked into a lather, and then toweled dry.)

Few of us have the perfect place to bathe a pet—it usually comes down to a choice between the kitchen sink and the bathtub or shower stall. Either way there's lots of spilled and splashed water and with the tub, a lot of bending over. A pet sink set up about waist high would be a lot more merciful. If you have stationary tubs in the utility or laundry room, basement, or garage, you can use these, too, but be sure that wherever you bathe your pet is well heated and free of drafts. You can bathe your dog outside, if it's a warm sunny day, but be sure to keep him on a leash throughout the process if you want to be sure the bath ends up a net gain.

In the sink or the tub, a sprayer attachment speeds up the whole process (which pets really appreciate). A sprayer attachment makes it easier to do a good job of rinsing without panicking a pet, which a blast from the shower head proper will surely do.

A rubber bath mat on the bottom of the tub or sink will make your pet a lot happier. From a pet's standpoint, it's bad enough being wet and soapy, without having this take place on a slippery, uncertain surface.

What Soap or Shampoo?

Don't ever think that when it comes to washing an animal, any old soap will do—chemicals are all too easily absorbed through the skin in the act of bathing. Never use dishwashing detergent or any household detergent to

shampoo pets, especially kittens or puppies. It's important to use not only a pet shampoo, but a shampoo designed especially for the type of pet you're washing. (Read the label!) Dog shampoos, for example, can be dangerous or deadly for cats, and people shampoo has the wrong pH for a dog or cat. Human shampoo, which is slightly acid, will give your pet an itchy skin and dry, flyaway hair that breaks easily. Pet shampoos not only have a somewhat alkaline "proper pH," but many of them are tearless and antistatic, too. Specially formulated pet shampoos are even available to enhance different coat colors such as black, brown, or bronze; shampoos for white dogs remove yellowish discolorations. There are pet conditioning shampoos, texture shampoos for rough-coated dogs like terriers, shampoos for pets with skin problems such as mange, oily dandruff, or eczema, and shampoos that neutralize and remove pet body odor.

There are creme rinses specially designed for pets, too, that do the same sorts of things the human creme rinses do: condition the hair and give it more body and make it glossier and more manageable. Pet creme rinses will also help prevent matting, and if you have a pet allergy problem you can even apply them and then not rinse them off. This will help keep the tiny skin flakes (dander) from flaking off your pet's body all over the house.

Never use turpentine, paint remover, or other strong solvents to remove tar or paint from an animal's coat. They can burn or irritate your pet's skin, or even poison him. Instead, soak the spot well with vegetable oil and leave it on overnight to allow the oil to penetrate. Then wash the area with pet shampoo and warm water. If that doesn't do it just cut out the patch of affected hair. It'll grow back soon enough.

Pet Bathing Psychology

A calm, pleasant, but *firm* manner assures your pet you know what you're doing and that escape is out of the question. Avoid abrupt movements that might alarm an already antsy pet. Some of the most effective pet bathers keep up a gentle, reassuring patter with their pet throughout the whole process, pouring on some praise with the water at the most harrowing moments. You may want to recruit a helper to help steady the pet (a cat, especially) through the initial skirmishes.

If your dog is likely to bolt, or a really stubborn resister, you might want to put him on a leash with a slip collar and have someone hold it tight above his head throughout the bath. If you attach your pet's leash to something to hold him while you bathe, make sure it's a towel bar, not the hot water faucet.

If you start getting a pet used to being bathed while he's young, he's much more likely to tolerate or even enjoy the process.

Right before the bath, make sure your pet has a chance to go outside for a walk or to the litter box. You don't want to have to worry about nature's call in the middle of the bath, and if you have to let a wet pet outside right after a bath you run the risk of chills and colds as well as rolls in the topsoil.

Brush your pet well to remove loose hair and any snarls, mats, or tangles, or the bath will only worsen them. Gently clean the inside of your pet's ears with a finger wrapped in a soft cloth moistened with mild soap and water. If you see excess wax, remove it with a cotton swab dipped in peroxide, rubbing alcohol, or commercial pet ear cleaning preparation. Don't probe deep into the ear with a cotton swab. To keep soap and water out, put cotton balls moistened with mineral oil or Vaseline in your pet's ears, and a dab of Vaseline in the corner of his eyes.

Basic Dog Bathing Procedure

If you're bathing a big dog, you may as well slip into your swimsuit now and admit that before it's over, you're going to be right in there beside him. Put several inches of lukewarm water in the tub before you start. Then lift your dog gently into the tub. Using a plastic pitcher, wet him down well with lukewarm water, from his neck to his tail. (Save the head for last, to postpone the panic button.)

If your pet has a flea problem, work up a ring of lather around his neck first to keep the fleas from fleeing to his head, then shampoo back from the neck toward the tail. If he doesn't have a flea problem, working from the tail end forward will scare him a little less.

Work up a good lather with your fingers (the superior tool for the purpose, all the experts agree) and massage your way down to the skin, but don't rub hard on or twist the dog's hair. With longhaired dogs, part the hair of the coat down the middle of the back and keep it parted during the bath to prevent hair breakage and tangling. "*Squeeze* the shampoo through the coat as if you're washing a delicate sweater," professional groomer Shirlee Kalstone says.

Pet bathers are inclined to do a big number on the back, chest, and shoulders, and forget about the tail, the rear end, the underside of the body, and the legs and feet. Remember that pet BO is strongest on bare skin areas and don't neglect them. Feet are best lifted up one at a time to wash. You can usually safe-

ly employ the dousing and lathering technique on the neck and up to behind the ears, but the face itself and muzzle are best approached (very cautiously) with a soapy sponge or washcloth.

You may want to repeat the shampooing process, after rinsing, if your pet is longhaired or dense-coated or very dirty. But resist the temptation to slack off a little on the rinsing. If you don't remove all the soap and shampoo you'll have a pet with a dull coat and itchy skin. (The old rule of thumb, "Rinse until you think it's all rinsed out, then rinse twice more" is a good one here.) As noted earlier, a hand sprayer can be a big help here. To get those last hard-to-reach spots you can refill the tub with a few inches of clean water and splash it up underneath your pet. A little vinegar or lemon juice added to the rinse water will cut the soap film, and a little baking soda added to it will make your pet's coat softer, shinier, and more odor-free.

We professionals dry paint rollers by spinning them, and that's exactly how dogs and cats get moisture off themselves. Dogs, especially, are going to shake when they're wet. You're not going to curb or eliminate the shaking instinct, so better they do it in a controlled area than in the hall or all over the house. In fact, their shaking will get the bulk of the water off a lot more efficiently than our soggy towels can manage. If you're bathing the animal inside, let him shake a few times after you finish rinsing—close the shower curtain or take cover behind a towel and move back and wait, he'll do it. (As soon as the dog is dry you can grab your squeegee and slick all the droplets off the shower walls in a wink.)

Then dry your pet off with a couple of big clean towels before you let him loose in the house. Be sure to keep him in a warm undrafty place for three to four hours, until he's completely dry. Dogs or cats with very heavy or double coats may take longer than that to dry fully—you may want to use a hair dryer (set on warm, not hot) to speed the process, or one of the high-speed dryers made specially for pets. If you use a dryer, brush your pet as you dry him, in the direction the hair naturally lays. If it's a warm sunny day, you could let a dog dry off outside—on a leash, or you'll be back to square one before you know it. (Don't forget to take the cotton out of your pet's ears when you're done.)

After he's dry, brush him well to restore the shine to his coat and remove the hair loosened by the bath. You'll notice by now that for all the struggling he did before and during, he seems prouder than you of the "after."

Cat Bathing Procedure

Cats in general seem intent on making it clear that they can keep *themselves* clean, thank you. So a cat bath is best approached as a two-person job. One person holds (restrains, grips, and attempts to soothe) while the other wets, soaps, and rinses. And watch those claws—a day or two before the bath might be a good time to clip your cat's claws.

A sink is better than a basin for the purpose—it can't be tipped over in the fray, even if your cat braces his feet against it. A two-compartment sink is better yet, because you can set the cat in one side and fill the other with clean lukewarm water for wetting, rinsing, etc. In cat bathing, faster is always bet-

ter, and it helps a lot to not have to wait for your pitcher to refill with rinse water. To help keep your cat steady during the bath, try folding a terry cloth towel and putting it in the bottom of the sink, or use an ordinary window screen in the bottom of a larger tub. Either of them will give a cat something to sink his claws into and anchor himself during the bath.

Grip the cat securely by the scruff of the neck and put your other hand under his chest, pointing him (and all those claws) *away* from you. Then set him gently in the empty sink; this will panic him less than an attempt to dunk him in a sink that's already filled with that awful water. Gently pour pitchers of the lukewarm water over him to wet him thoroughly, then apply some shampoo

and work up a good lather. If you're using a tangle-removing shampoo, make sure you saturate every mat and tangle with it. Cat faces, too, are best cleaned with a washcloth. Be especially sure to rinse a cat well; you can be sure they'll be licking themselves vigorously after a bath. Then wrap kitty in a big clean towel and dry him off as much as you can before you put him in a warm place to finish drying.

De-Flea Your Life

Fleas often go unseen, but they rarely go unfelt, and a single animal can be infested by a hundred or more of the nasty little buggers. Most flea species stick to their own particular host, but if deprived of its usual dinner a flea will attack other warm-blooded animals, and humans obviously aren't exempt. These tiny bloodsuckers can take big bites, causing skin irritation and even anemia. They can also transmit bacterial and viral infections, and a pet can catch tapeworms from a flea if he happens to swallow it.

If you're infested, the only remedy is ridding your life of the tiny rascals. But this isn't a matter of sprinkling a little flea powder on your pet from time to time. It's a full-scale war. Fleas don't *live* on animals, they only jump up on them to feed from time to time. They make their home, and spend 90 percent of their time, in carpets, rugs, bedding, floor cracks, and damp sheltered areas anywhere in the house and yard. So to get rid of fleas you have to treat not merely your pet but his whole surroundings, and you have to use measures that will kill not only the adult fleas but the immature stages such as larvae. Since no product can yet manage to kill flea

REEEAOOOOOW!!

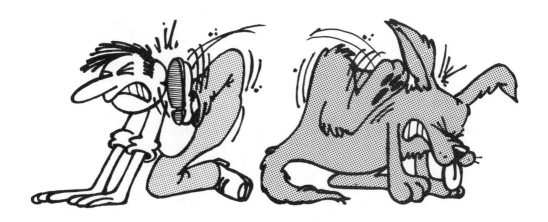

eggs, you have to keep treating till all the existing eggs have hatched and you've destroyed all the future crops of fleas and broken the infestation chain.

A flea elimination campaign is indeed a battle plan—you have a lot of ground to cover and timing is critical—you can't skip any step, and you must do them all at once, within a single day. This means: treat the pet himself (*all* your pets) with a flea shampoo, dip, or flea combing. Treat the entire inside of the house and the inside of the car and your pet's bedding and roosting places with a spray or fogger, and spray the yard. (Don't let your freshly treated pets back into the house or yard till you've finished treating those areas.) Repeat the process as often as the labels of the preparations you're using tell you to.

Then you have to stay on the alert for reinfestation from animals and areas outside all your treated areas. You can do this all yourself, or have an exterminator do much or all of it. But thoroughness and tenacity are the name of this game, for sure. Don't do half the steps and neglect the other half, or only attack fleas in fits and starts—this is one of the surest ways to have your pet end up with fleabite allergy.

Insecticides

It's easy to be confused by the incredible array of flea products and preparations available, from sprays to dusts to dips to shampoos to foggers. The thing to realize is that when it comes to flea-control products, "There's no such thing as a perfect 10."

Before choosing a flea product, take your pet to the vet and have his level of infestation checked out, or take a close look at him yourself. When you part his hair, does it look like crosstown traffic, or do you have to dig to find a flea or two? Do you get five flea bites on the ankle every time you walk across the rug in your stocking feet? Do you need the extra-strong products dispensed only by vets, or that can only be used by professional exterminators? Fleas, like other insects, become resistant to insecticides over time—your vet will know which are likely to work best in your area at this particular point in time.

Never use dog flea killers on cats, or vice versa—their systems and chemical tolerances are entirely different. Read the label of any flea product carefully before applying it. Insecticide application is the *last* place you ever want to consider acting on the popular assumption that more is better—*always* follow directions exactly and don't use more than one kind of chemical flea remedy on your pet at once.

SYSTEMICS

are flea-killing chemicals such as Proban and Ectoral, given by injection or in pill form. These keep a low level of insecticide in a pet's bloodstream or body at all times, so a flea that bites the animal will die. But many pet experts feel that systemics subject an animal to some serious possible side-effects, for a control that works only after the flea's bitten the animal, and only effectively controls a problem if it's caught early, before the flea population proliferates. Systemics should only be used when recommended by a vet and under his or her supervision, and they should *never* be used on cats.

SPRAYS

for use directly on a pet kill fleas quickly, but cats and dogs don't take the hiss and chill of aerosol quite as much for granted as we do, so you may need a helper to hold the animal while you do the spraying. The considerably quieter pump sprays are a lot less unsettling to a pet. You can also minimize scariness by spraying the brush, instead of the pet, or by spraying behind your hand as it moves over your pet's body. Brush the hair backwards and fluff it up as you spray. Avoid spraying a pet's face and genitals and try to keep him from licking himself till the spray has a chance to dry.

When you're handling and applying sprays and other flea-killers, wear rubber gloves and clothes that cover your arms and legs, because many insecticides can be absorbed through the skin. Remove and wash the clothes when you're done; don't eat, drink, or smoke after applying such products until you've washed your hands well. Keep all pets (and children) well out of the way when you're applying the remedies, and be sure there's enough ventilation to disperse toxic fumes—flea-killers are poison.

POWDERS

are messy and time-consuming to apply and somewhat shortlived in their effect, but they're generally safer and more easily tolerated by pets than other means of flea control. Many powders contain insecticides such as pyrethrum or rotenone that act fast but may only stun or temporarily paralyze some of the fleas, so be sure to apply powders in a place where you can vacuum up or hose away the fleas that fall off the animal. There are even powders that use things like silica gel to dry the fleas up, or diatomaceous earth to grind holes in their hard outer shells.

Set your pet on an old towel or sheet of newspaper before you start. Apply the powder over your pet's whole body, but don't overdo it and stay away from eyes and the inside of ears. Work it through the hair all the way down to the skin, paying attention to flea havens such as around the outside of the ears, the hindquarters, and the base of the tail. Don't forget the legs, and even between the toes.

Leave the powder on for about ten minutes and then brush or comb it out.

A FLEA BAG

is a cloth bag you tuck your kitty in so that the powder can more surely engulf him (every part of his body, that is, not his head, which stays outside the bag). Commercially available versions include the Kit-Cat Flea Bag and the Kitty Car-e-er. There are also Velcro-sealing mitts you fill with powder so you can powder your pet as you pet him.

A FLEA COMB

has thin metal teeth so closely spaced that even our agile and slender friend the flea can't evade them. Comb your pet thoroughly all over, starting with the head and working back, using a good flea powder. Or use a special comb with hollow teeth that dispenses insecticide as you comb. Some of the best-respected brands of this type of flea comb are Fleamaster and Twinco, and there are also brushes such as the Brushette with hollow rubber or nylon bristles that work on the same basic principle.

Hand-picking fleas is probably the most demanding (it calls for a sharp eye and quick reflexes) and sporting approach—you simply comb your pet till you see a flea and then grab it between thumb and index finger. No matter how hard you grip it there, be assured you haven't killed it, so drop it into hot water or alcohol. (Or, the most satisfying approach—into a fishtank so you can watch the thrashing flea be picked neatly off the surface by your favorite goldfish.)

DIPS

are one of the surest ways of killing fleas and ticks on an animal, especially a heavily infested one, and most dips will provide a good measure of protection for a week or two or even three afterwards. But dips are strong chemicals, so check with your vet about the advisibility of using one on the age and type of pet you have in mind. Despite the name, you don't have to dunk your pet in a dip—you apply it by sponging or pouring it over him after he's been wetted down with water, such as right after a bath. And you don't rinse a dip off, you let it dry right on the coat after squeezing off the excess. A dip is usually mixed up from concentrate; be sure to follow the dilution directions on the package.

And since dips are one of the more powerful flea treatments always be sure to do your dipping in a well-ventilated room.

When you apply a dip, stay away from your pet's eyes, mouth, and nose as well as any open sores. Use cool or lukewarm water to mix the dip as further insurance against overdose—the hotter the water, the more easily chemicals can be absorbed through the skin.

Cats are about as fond of dipping as they are of bathing, but if you can manage to dip your cat (it might be better to have the vet or groomer do it) be sure to use a dip specifically for cats. If you want to tackle dipping a cat yourself see "Defleaing the Cat" by Valerie Matthews in the August 1980 issue of *Cat Fancy*.

FLEA SHAMPOOS

are much milder than dips and must be used faithfully about once a week or they won't keep your pet free of fleas. Brush your pet well before shampooing to remove loose hair and mats and lather up his neck at the very start to keep fleas from running to his head for cover. Be sure to lather his whole body, and do the hindquarters especially well—and leave the lather on as long as the directions say to, to be sure the chemical has time to work. Thorough rinsing is important here, and a spray attachment will be a real help.

FLEA COLLARS

—the easy way out? When flea collars—an outgrowth of the famous No Pest Strip, by the way—first came out, we all tended to think that here at last was a simple, neat, clean, effective, one-step way to deal with the problem once and for all. But while flea collars can be a useful aid, they are only an *aid* in controlling fleas and ticks on pets. Remem-

(Continued on page 94)

Flea Hideout Hotspot Checklist

Many pet owners spend a lot of time and money trying to control fleas on their pets, yet they do nothing about the pets' environment. Yet fleas spend considerably more time off a pet than on it. They don't live on animals—they get a quick meal and jump down from the dinner ta-ble. At least ninety percent of their time is spent away from the host. As soon as fleas are killed on the pet, more jump on. For a flea-control program to be effective, you have to treat both the animal and his whole environment.

These are places fleas hide:

1. **attic**
2. **under edges of throw rugs**
3. **lower part of draperies**
4. **beds**
5. **baseboards**

6. walls to a height of about one foot
7. bird or rodent nests
8. shady areas outdoors
9. the inside of the car
10. bare dirt or sand
11. crawl space under house
12. vicinity of all entranceways
13. porch
14. grass or weeds
15. basement
16. carpeting
17. upholstered furniture
18. under furniture cushions
19. corners
20. edges of carpet
21. pet's bed and bedding
22. floor cracks
23. cracks and crevices (and other moist sheltered areas)
24. small holes that lead from outside to inside
25. hard floors
26. sandbox
27. windowsills
28. other favorite pet napping places indoors
29. doghouse and under doghouse
30. under outbuildings and sheds, and in the garage
31. favorite pet napping spots outdoors

ber, the fleas on the pet itself are only a small part of the story, and a collar only works on the fleas on the pet. And there are some limitations and potential problems in how collars accomplish that.

Flea collars are usually plastic collars impregnated with an insecticide that's steadily released in small amounts and gradually dispersed over the hair of the pet's whole body. They work more slowly than other forms of flea control—it may take several days after you put a collar on, before it really does its thing. The collar (and the greatest force of flea-killing) is near a pet's sensitive head, whereas the flea problem is usually worst on the hindquarters and around the tail. And pets can develop allergic or toxic reactions to a flea collar, so you have to watch any pet wearing one closely for redness, sores, or hair loss around the neck, or more serious symptoms such as listlessness or loss of coordination and appetite.

Flea collars are more effective on small, shorthaired dogs than large shaggy ones, and they're almost useless on longhaired cats.

Never put a flea collar on tight; there should be at least an inch, or two finger widths of space between the neck and the collar. A breakaway style is safer, should your pet ever get hung up somewhere. Use only one flea collar at a time on any animal, and never use a flea collar on pups or kittens under two months old, or on a sick or nursing pet, or a pet with no fleas. Many experts recommend airing out a flea collar for two or three days before putting it on your pet.

Be aware, too, that if many flea collars get wet they release more chemical than they're supposed to—so remove a flea collar as soon as you can, if your pet gets drenched or goes swimming.

Many pet owners hedge the risks of flea collars by using them for a few days or short periods only, then storing them in an airtight container in a cool place until the next use. Or they use flea tags—which attach to a pet's regular collar like a license tag—instead of flea collars. A tag is smaller and doesn't come in as close contact with the pet's skin as a collar. The "isolated" flea collars, which have the insecticide-releasing layer sealed within a regular collar, are also less likely to irritate a pet's neck.

Check the expiration date on the box when you buy a collar. (If it has no such date, how shopworn does the package look?) Likewise, collars are often left on too long, past the point of effectiveness. Again, check the box—many collars are designed to work for three months or less, though there are some that work for nearly a year.

All in all, collars serve best as a measure of protection against reinfestation from areas and animals outside the bounds of your home grounds flea-killing campaign. Perhaps a better way to guard against reinfestation, after you've rid the pet and his quarters of fleas, is to make a practice of treating him each time he comes inside, as Gwen Bohnenkamp suggests. This is a lot easier than it sounds. All you do is put a blanket in the animal's bed or crate, or in some quiet corner where he likes to idle away the day; liberally sprinkle the blanket with flea powder; and then train your pet to walk straight to his blanket and lie down there for a couple of minutes each time he comes inside. Once a week, wash or vacuum the blanket well and add fresh flea powder. You can also give your pet a flea combing after he's been out in untreated territory.

Treating the Place

You can hire an exterminating service to spray inside and outside the house every few months, or you can do it yourself, using flea-killing sprays, aerosol bombs, or foggers. (Sprays and foggers can reach every little crack and corner better than powders.) A professional exterminator does have the advantage of knowing all the favorite flea hiding places and of knowing how to get maximum kill.

If you decide to do the spraying yourself, try to choose (your vet can help you here) a spray that's effective on as many stages of the flea life cycle as possible, yet as safe as possible for the pets you have in your house and the many different kinds of household surfaces you'll have to spray it on. A flea-spraying operation is going to cover a lot of territory: floors, carpets, upholstered furniture, drapes, the lower parts of walls, anywhere pets lay or climb, baseboards, edges, cracks, nooks and crannies, and even the insides of closets and underneath furniture cushions and between the mattress and box spring. If you don't cover all this, the fleas will just jump to the unsprayed places and continue to thrive and multiply. Be sure to clean well—vacuum, sweep, and declutter—before you spray, to get all the debris out of the way of the flea-killing agent.

Don't let any pets back into sprayed areas till they're fully dry and aired out, and be sure to repeat the spraying as often as the label instructs.

FOGGING

is an easy way to achieve complete coverage of an area, but it's really a more practical treatment for flying insects than for fleas, which spend most of their time on the ground. A good thorough spraying is as effective, and less wasteful, for the purpose.

But if you want to fog your fleas away, a vet or pet store or pet catalog is the best place to buy a fogger for use around pets. Be sure to evacuate all pets (including fish and birds) as well as their food and water dishes before fogging. You can't do one room this week and another room next week, because the fleas will just run from room to room. Put a fogger on each floor or in each room; there are mini-foggers such as those made by Mycodex and Daltek that are just the right size for a single room. Get all pets and people out of there, go to the park or something for the day, and fog the whole place. (One good thing to do with the pets is to take them to a professional groomer for an expertly-administered dip while you're fogging the fleas out of the premises.) Here, too, you want to unclutter as much as possible first, vacuum all carpeting and upholstered furniture, open all the closet doors, and lift the skirts of sofas and the dust ruffles of beds, so the fog can reach everywhere. Air the house well before reentry, and don't be tempted to move anything back in sooner than the label says.

To clear a flea infestation, fogging, too, will have to be repeated as often as the label instructs.

FLEA TRAPS

work because fleas, like other insects, are attracted to light (and in this case will jump to it). If you don't want to use chemicals to battle the flea problem you can rig a lamp with a low-wattage bulb (not more than 60 watts) so that it shines all night on a shallow pan or light-colored dish of water set on the floor of a flea-infested room. Be sure to add about a tablespoon of dish detergent to the water in the pan to soften the water surface so the fleas will be sure to sink. And it's not a bad idea to secure the lamp at the base to a 2-foot square of plywood or the like.

This method is 100 percent environmentally safe, as well as cheap. Keep the trap in operation in a given area till you don't find any dead fleas in the morning, then move it to another part of the house. But return it to each flea-infested room within three weeks to be sure to catch the next crop of developing fleas. If your house is badly infested you may want to set up several traps.

A somewhat more sophisticated version of this device, that uses a piece of special sticky paper to catch the fleas, is available from Happy Jack, Inc. of Snow Hill, North Carolina, and according to the manufacturer "It will control fleas in the home year round without pesticides, chemicals, or the need to evacuate the home to exterminate pests. Used over a period of several weeks, the trap is guaranteed to show significant results and achieve flea control throughout the home. 'I caught 116 fleas the first night and the trap continued to kill fleas until they got smaller and smaller,' explained one user. 'I realized I was destroying a second generation of fleas before they reached maturity. After 35 days, the flea count was negligible.' "

DON'T FORGET THE YARD,

the garage, and the doghouse in your flea elimination program. Spraying is usually the most efficient way to treat a large area like a yard, and you can use a small power or compressed-air sprayer or a spray attachment on the hose. Or hire an exterminator. Here, again, you want to clean up and declutter before you spray (in this case yard litter, lawn clippings, leaves, piles of rotting lumber and like debris). Use a product specifically for flea-killing and cover the area thoroughly, paying special attention to the lower parts and underneath things.

Yard treatment may not have to be repeated (check the label of the chemical you're using) unless you have a reinfestation. In that case the whole flea battle campaign will have to be waged over again.

Cleanliness: One of the Best Protections Against Fleas

Cleaning your home and its contents, the grounds, as well as the animal itself is the ultimate enemy of fleas. If no places are left available or untreated, if they can't comfortably breed and reproduce, they won't.

1. **The vacuum:** *Frequent and thorough vacuuming is one of the best ways to reduce the flea population—a good vacuum with a strong, properly adjusted beater bar will get a lot of the fleas and their larvae right where they live. The top priorities: carpet and upholstered furniture, cracks and corners and crevices, and around baseboards and other woodwork. Don't forget the inside of the car, if your pet is a frequent passenger.*

When you're flea-vacuuming, be sure to use a disposable bag and dispose of it, well sealed in a plastic bag, right after you finish. (Better yet, incinerate it, if burning is allowed in your area.) Or if you must use a cloth bag, put some flea powder—or the leftover piece from a flea collar—inside the bag before you start. That way you won't have fleas hatching in the bag, hopping out the tube and out of the garbage can. There are a number of rug and carpet powders made to be applied to, then vacuumed up from, a carpet to kill fleas. Be cautious with these, since flea-killers are poison and a certain amount of dust is always redistributed into the air when you're vacuuming. Carpet powders will also leave a dulling residue over time. If you do use a flea-killing carpet powder or spray, make sure it's one from a veterinary supply house or pet product manufacturer.

The help a vacuum can be in flea control is another incentive to teach your pet not to fear vacuuming, so you can vacuum the fleas and flea eggs right off him, too. (If you'd like to make your own flea zapping mini-vacuum much less likely to scare your pet, Phil Philcox will tell you how to do it for less than $20, using an aquarium pump, some plastic tubing, and a plastic bag. See the July 1983 issue of Cat Fancy.)

2. **When you shampoo your carpet** have it steam cleaned by a strong truck-mounted unit. In steam cleaning, the water is heated to 170° and applied under great pressure, so it's hard for fleas to survive.

3. **The pet's bed** and any place else he beds down are the places you're surest to find developing fleas. Wash the pet's bedding in hot water and strong detergent at least once a week. If he sleeps on disposable bedding, change it often and discard the old bedding in a sealed plastic bag. Sprinkle some flea powder in your pet's bed every few weeks or include the pet's bed in your spraying campaign if you use a flea spray. Don't forget to also treat any human bedding your pet comes in contact with, as well as furniture, area rugs, etc., he lays on.

4. **Eliminate the cracks,** crevices, and dark moist corners in your home where fleas and their larvae live. Caulk and fill any small holes or gaps or cracks, any possible places and passages for them to get in from outside. Eliminate all these and you'll be amazed at what you can accomplish with prevention.

5. **Use a good flea powder on your pet when you groom** and you'll add real help with flea control to the other advantages of grooming your pet. Put the combings in a plastic bag with a little flea powder and seal the bag before discarding it. And spray your grooming tools from time to time with a little flea spray to eliminate the fugitives that may be hanging on.

AAAAAAH!

JUMP!

RUN FOR YER LIVES!

CHAPTER 6

Pets Do the Darndest Things

A pet's determination and agility should never be underestimated, as an experience I had when I was eight years old taught me.

My parents had butchered a prime steer, and selected a gorgeous roast to send to our neighbors. Mom put the roast on a large plate, spread a fresh dishcloth over it, and said, "Now Donny, take this over to Rose and Mel's and leave the cover on so the flies and dust won't get into it."

I knocked at the neighbor's front door, and as I wanted to make the presentation as astounding as possible, I snatched off the dishcloth and held that huge hunk of meat up proudly as Rose opened the door. The second I did this, a big barnyard cat that I hadn't seen stir in weeks sprang thirteen feet and snatched the roast from the plate. He hit the ground with the meat still gripped in his jaws, and Rose and I watched as the six-pound roast was dragged across the gravel and manure of the barnyard and disappeared into the bushes to be consumed.

Since then, I've never underestimated an animal's ability or desire to jump, be it up cliffs or tables or counters.

Pets Jump to It

If you're going to have a pet, then the physical environment has to be of a strength, quality, and design that can handle it. Small pets usually do less damage than big pets. A St. Bernard can dent a car if left alone with it in the garage. A big dog needs a big walkway, and a big tail can easily brush objets d'art from the coffee table. Arranging and decorating your home to fit the size of your pet is much easier than teaching your pet to be small. Go for sturdy tables and lamps instead of the spindly-legged kind, so bumps and vibrations won't be catastrophes. Eliminate loose and dangling electrical cords, or strategically position them so they won't be tripped over, chewed on, or pulled on to pull something down. Windowsills are naturally attractive because of the warm sunlight and the view of the great outdoors, so don't put things on sills or on the edges of shelves or mantels where they're almost sure to be knocked off.

Design things so that even if a pet does get up and on, they can't do any damage. Tile, marble, and glass sills and tabletops are sleek, cool, and can't be hurt. Plastic laminates, too, are almost pet-proof, and very easy to clean. If your houseplants and flower arrangements are in heavy pots or vases (avoid the light little baskets and storklike plant stands), they'll be less likely to be toppled by a passing or climbing animal.

Cats are curious by nature and born climbers, so use a curio cabinet with glass doors to protect your ceramic chicken collection (saves on dusting, too). It's unrealistic to expect a pet to tiptoe around little stands precariously balancing precious bric-a-brac. Pets,

like us, can resist everything except temptation. Don't tempt your animal with frilly decorations. Dangling things will drive a playful cat crazy and pets have even more trouble than children understanding: "Don't touch!" Tassels and hanging macrames and heavily fringed curtains are natural playthings to a pet.

Holiday ornaments can be a big pet problem. Don't put the ornaments that have been in the family for generations on the lower branches. Instead, put some unbreakables down there and tie them on securely. Tinsel is dangerous for pets, too—they can strangle or choke on it.

You can train a pet to not climb—it takes time and patience, but can be done. Start when it's young and be consistent. The squirt bottle trick is workable here, if you catch them in the act. A good firm "No!" is another convincer. You can also put your pet on a leash, watch him, catch him in the act of going up on something, and then jerk the leash hard and say *"No!"*

When you correct a pet for jumping up and get it down off something, take it easy. If your cat's claws are caught in the doily and you pluck him off the end table, whose fault is it when the vase crashes to the floor? Often more damage is done in the retaliation than the initial transgression. People and furniture get scratched, and things get broken and spilled when we react violently to our pet's misbehavior.

Restricting the areas of the house the pet is allowed in is an obvious solution. Keep the animal in areas where no climbing can be done, or can't cause any problem if it is.

Tempt them away. You can build or buy a pet "swing set" with all kinds of goodies to keep your animal occupied and out of mischief. Place some little rewards on the legal climbing place and have a soft cushy perch at the top. And offer some sturdy active toys as alternatives. If pets, like children, have their own toys to play with they'll be less likely to tamper with yours. If you have young children and are in the child-proofing channel, you're already halfway pet-proofed.

Pets Jumping Up on Counters or Tables

This is usually a food-related problem. Feeding your pet in only one place will help condition him to leave other food alone. And don't ask for trouble. Don't leave food lying or defrosting on the counter or table or in the sink when you're not around. Leaving dirty dishes lying out is almost as bad.

Never feed your pet from the table or give him leftovers. Remove him from the area while you're eating.

Discourage with the Scat bottle, or other correction technique of your choice, but be sure to stick with it and be consistent. Don't squirt or shoo him away today and find his saucer-slurping cute tomorrow. Harden your heart. If he succeeds in swiping something before your very eyes, don't let him eat it—even if it does mean a totally wasted rock cornish hen. (Do you want to *reward* him for his transgression?)

BOOBY TRAP

Set a piece of cardboard on the counter so it overhangs the edge by three or four inches, and stack three or more shake cans in a pyramid on top of the cardboard. When your pet jumps up on the counter he'll land on the edge of the cardboard, causing the cans to crash down.

You'll probably have to do this setup more than once, and maybe even put the cardboard and cans the whole length of the counter, but after those cans come down a time or two, even the most nonchalant feline will think twice before jumping up there again. Another tactic is to pop some balloons near your pet so he'll develop an aversion to them. Then the mere sight of a balloon on the counter will be a deterrent.

Since cats hate to step on anything sticky, some people use two-sided sticky tape on the counter (you may have to use a lot of it). You could also set some upside-down mousetraps under sheets of newspaper taped to the counter.

Dogs Jumping on People

Any moment now, that's it, here she comes, through the gate. It's Aunt Elsie in her Sunday best—peach jacket, satin blouse, fox boa, sheerest hose, flowered hat, and wow, white gloves—go meet her, boy!

A muddied and crumpled Aunt Elsie rings the bell. "Oh my word, Elsie! I'm so sorry. I thought that dog was tied up out back! Come on in and let's get you cleaned up."

That's the last we'll see of Aunt Elsie for a while. A jumping dog can make a real mess and even be a safety threat, especially to children.

The only way to greet a pet is with all six feet firmly on the ground—your two and his four. Short of teaching your dog to wipe his feet and trim his nails, there's no way to lessen the impact of a jumper, but there are a number of ways to train your pet not to jump. First you must make the decision: to allow jumping or not to allow it. Your entire household must make the decision, because the key to successful training is consistency.

As the pet experts point out, the problem of jumping comes about because the dog was allowed or encouraged to do it

as a pup. Remember when you brought home that little ball of fur and nuzzled it to your face and snuggled it under your chin? Well, your pet remembers, too. He's found that warmth and affection center up around your face—that's where your voice, that he's learned to love and obey, comes from, too.

The very least you should do is tell your guests what to expect before they enter your dog's domain. Let them choose whether to risk their new suit or not. This courtesy to the jumpee is a basic of pet etiquette. If he chooses not to risk it, then make alternate plans—go out for coffee or excuse yourself and shut Rover in a "safe room."

Any of the following training methods are best practiced over and over in the same way. It may take a month or more to change his behavior, but you must outlast your pet!

- *Hold a book out and down in front of you, in both hands, so the jumper will bump his nose as he comes up. Or grab your pet's two front paws and hold them at your sides. If he knows he'll get stuck there, after a few times, he'll think twice about jumping up.*

- *Attach a short leash or cord to his collar (he should wear this only when you're present), and when he jumps pull down hard and to the right to throw him off balance and say "No—off." If the dog you're training is a large one, you may have to have a helper handle the leash while you serve as bait. You can also squirt the jumping pet with a squirt bottle or rattle a shake can at him and say "No—off."*

- *Antijump harnesses are made by several companies and work by restraining the hind legs. They keep a dog from jumping over a fence, on furniture, or on people. Once the dog finds out the futility of jumping, the harness can be removed.*

- An obedience-trained dog may be told to "Sit-stay" to calm the excitement every time a guest comes to your door. Practice leaving the house and returning, and when you enter command the dog to sit.

- No one in your household should welcome your dog if he's jumping up on them. When you come home it excites your dog, and encourages him to jump. So instead of making a fuss when you walk in the door, give him only a mild greeting and save the play for a little later. Kneel to bring yourself down to your pet's level when you want to relate to him, instead of encouraging him to come up to yours. Praise and pet him only when all four feet are on the ground.

- If your pet's nails are clipped short and filed smooth there's less chance of injury to your furniture, your skin, and your ninety-dollar dress.

- Many dogs jump up on people as a simple matter of excess energy. See that such a pet, especially, gets regular vigorous exercise—it'll help calm him down.

Two often-heard suggestions for stopping a jumper are kneeing the dog in the chest as he jumps and stepping on his back toes. These are unnecessarily cruel methods that could damage your relationship with your pet. Better to invest some time and patience in your animal to discourage the behavior before it occurs, rather than to reprimand or punish your pet when he can't understand why you're doing it.

Bear in mind that shouting or raising your arms often excites a dog into more jumping. And holding things out at arm's length to him is *training* him to jump up. Also, if you allow your pet on the furniture, he's more likely to jump up on people.

Cats Jumping on People

It's too late to inform your guest of your cat's cute habit of jumping up on people after it leaps on his lap and his allergy renders him apoplectic. As the proud owner, you're likely to be more tolerant of your cat snagging your last pair of pantyhose, because you've chosen to keep a pet. But a person who dislikes cats may consider it a minor catastrophe.

In training a cat not to jump on people you must be persistent. You can try squirting it with your spray bottle or rattling a shake can; many cats also respond to a "Psssst-pssst" vocal reprimand.

Though you will come across an occasional cat who delights in walking right up a person's body to his shoulder or leaping onto a shoulder from a nearby tree, cats don't usually jump up on people and claw them. Cats may, however, "knead" when they're feeling content. It looks just like someone kneading bread, except that cats use their paws (and claws, usually into someone's lap or leg). Kittens knead when they're nursing and many an adult cat kneads and purrs when he's feeling pleased.

Disciplining a cat for kneading is impractical as well as unfriendly. It's like asking a child not to smile when he's happy. He might also turn from kneading to more troublesome habits like chewing. A better solution to kneading is to put a towel between you and the cat. Or give kitty his own old blanket or pillow to knead and suck to his heart's content.

If you feel the claws coming out in the kneading behavior, you can gently remove the cat from your lap, being careful to disengage your clothing from the claws before pushing him away. Avoid reacting quickly or shoving and panicking the cat, so you won't get scratched or snagged.

If snagged pantyhose are your pet peeve, there is a solution for this. PurFit Panty Hose, guaranteed not to run. Most pantyhose are made with a slip-stitch, but these are made with a special lockstitch and are available in twenty-eight colors. If you're wondering why these aren't at the corner store, I don't know, but they are available through the mail from Raenell's Marketing, P.O. Drawer 185609, Fort Worth, TX 76181.

Pets Tracking in Dirt and Mud

Out West where I live, it's said that a crack Indian tracker can trace a rabbit's trail over solid rock. Most of us have no trouble at all tracking our pets across our kitchen floors and carpets. The Indian has to call on keen instinct and skill—all we have to do is look!

While our pets are outside exploring, they pick up all manner of debris which seems to only be dislodged once they're inside the house. It's not just the bits of grit, sand, and gravel that dirty things up inside—pets track in things like mud, salt, tar, doo-doo, grass, burrs, and anything else that can stick to them. And wet feet, once in the house, dry off into dust and dirt particles. So drying off both your and your pet's feet before entering your home is important, winter and summer.

Cut Track-Ins at Their Source

We professionals call this "eliminating the watering hole" (or mud hole, in this case). That tracked-in stuff has most likely come from somewhere close by. Let's look at some ways to stop the problem right at the source.

1. ***Close off under things.*** *This means under the house, under the porch, under stairs, benches, workbenches, planters, etc. Animals in search of shade, privacy, or a cozy den will seek out these places, which are generally bare dirt (because nothing grows there) and strewn with greasy bones and dead moles and grubbed garbage.*

2. ***Cover up*** *the bare ground in your yard with grass, gravel, or concrete, especially under and around hose spigots or water use areas and right by the entryways. Traversing bare dirt really lodges trackables in pets' paws.*

3. ***Seal up outside storage.*** *It's amazing how much stuff we store outside—including the garbage. Our junk is really the most intriguing thing we own, as far as animals are concerned. Lids and covers are cheap and easy to use—though they might keep you from becoming a famous Indian tracker!*

4. ***Clean up.*** *People will at least try to avoid stepping in things, but an animal will track in anything it encounters outside, so the cleanliness of the immediate outdoors will determine the mess indoors. If oil is leaking on the driveway, the cat will track it into the house. If the sidewalk is plastered with mud, soon the entryway will be.*

If your grounds are cleaned up, your cleaning will be cut down.

5. ***Rake up.*** *Get a lawn mower that bags the grass so that cut grass isn't lying all over the yard and blown onto sidewalks for people and pets to pick up on their wet feet and drag in.*

6. ***Install professional "knockoff" mats.*** *Mats are inexpensive, attractive, sound-absorbing, and a powerful cleaning prevention tool. They also make your entryway safer. The bristly surface of an artificial turf mat will tickle the dirt out of the pet's paws, and the magnetic surface of the inside mat will pull the dust off. A 3×5-foot mat both inside and outside each door assures enough steps on the matting to do a good job of pulling off grit and loose litter.*

7. ***Entry training*** *can be another cure for tracking in. You can train a dog to go to a specific spot as soon as he comes in and wait to be toweled off. This training is easy—just have a towel handy, and set a mat in a place close by the pet entryway. Then catch your pet as he comes in and make him stay or sit on the mat. (You might even reward him with a little love or a treat, as long as he does stay.) The longer he stays, even if you don't towel him off, the more he dries off and transfers trackable stuff onto the surface of the mat.*

You can even design or make a little nook for the purpose by the door the animal enters (in most households the pets make the majority of their entrances and exits from the same door).

Take Matters into Your Own Hands

With all the stuff that can be found on the ground today, it's important to wipe your pet's feet off as soon as he comes in. Road salt can be toxic to a pet, and if you don't clean it off he'll do it himself while grooming, possibly ingesting a dangerous amount. Mud, too, is a good medium for bacteria and fungi to flourish in, so it can help transmit diseases to your pet or others in the house.

Professional trainers recommend you start getting an animal used to "handling"—whether a puppy or an adult—as soon as you bring him home. While petting and reassuring him, first touch his head and back (the nonthreatening areas). Then pick up a front foot and put it down just the way you would if you were teaching a dog to "give a paw." Pick up the other front foot for just a minute, then put it down. After you do both front feet, then pick up a back foot and put it back down. Two hours later play the game again, this time picking up each foot and squeezing it a little, then putting it right back down. At any sign of panic or uneasiness from the animal, stop what you're doing and begin again later. Use treats, toys, anything you can to make it an upbeat experience. You want to get him used to your handling, to rubbing his feet, and to going in between his toes to get out any crud. Clean all foreign substances from your pet's paws, and check in the long hair many dogs have between their toes for mud, matted hair, and pebbles. Trimming the excess hair around the foot on shaggy breeds will also cut down on tracking in.

You can't really entry train cats, but when you let the cat in you can scoop him up and put him on a towel on a counter or something and feed him a little goody and get him purring, then gently take his feet one by one and rub them off with a paper towel or a damp washcloth.

Last but not least there are dog boots. After my experience trying to sort and apply boots to six small kids, I'll pass up this possibility. But if footwear for Fifi sounds like the answer to you, I wish you luck and patience.

MUD
If your pet does manage to track in mud, the secret is to wait until it dries. Brush the dry mud loose, then wipe or vacuum it up. Spray some all-purpose cleaner solution on the residue that remains, let it sit for a few seconds, then blot or wipe it up. Very little soil will penetrate a carpet made of nylon or other synthetic fibers. Natural fibers like wool are a little more absorbent. Using a soil retardant on the carpet will make spills and stains much easier to deal with.

TAR
Tracked-in tar, too, is simple. Tar and tarlike substances have a solvent base, so waterbased cleaners won't touch them. But dry-cleaning fluid, such as Carbona or Energine, blotted carefully on a tar stain will dissolve and release it, even if it's old. Always scrape up as much of the spot as you can before applying the cleaning fluid, and use a white cloth so you'll know whether the fabric is bleeding.

Pets Scratching
Few things come more naturally to cats and dogs and other pets than scratching. Cats, the most frequent offenders, scratch to remove the old layers of nail from their claws, to stretch and exercise themselves, and to leave little messages for their fellow cats with the scent glands on their front paws. Dogs scratch as part of their bedding down routine, to make nests for imaginary puppies, when they're in heat, and when they want to get in, out, or away.

But it costs—in time, money, and lost tempers—if the wrong thing is scratched, too often and too deeply.

Since breeding out the instinct and need to scratch is about as likely in the near future as getting us humans to quit it, there are some other measures that can be taken.

Solution #1: A Post

For cats, put up a scratching post. These work by the principle of diversion—they let a pet scratch something that won't be damaged. It's the same principle used on the ranch and farm. Cows, for example, will scratch against and tear up barn siding, fences, and machinery. So the farmer plants a rough post for them to scratch on and they take their pleasures out on it instead of the other surfaces.

You can buy a scratching post or build your own—you don't have to be a mechanical wizard to do it. Just be sure the post has a large, heavy base to prevent it from tipping over. And make sure it's securely attached to the base— if the cat accidentally knocks the post over while using it, he may never want to use it again.

You don't want a fluffy-wuffy post. A harsh, scratchy surface like sisal rope is far more attractive to a cat than carpeting of any kind. A cat wants *resistance* when he scratches something, and carpet can't provide it. Besides, a carpeted post may teach him that it's okay to claw carpet. The *backing* of the average carpet, on the other hand, is rough enough to have real claw appeal. Burlap or very highly textured fabric is good, too. Cork, log with bark, and rough-cut wood posts work, but are going to leave crumbs and splinters around.

The post should be at least a foot taller than your cat stretched up on tippy-toe. But a floor-to-ceiling post will be a lot more stable than a very tall free-standing post. A couple of sturdy cat perches or cozy cat cubbyholes will enhance the appeal of a big tall post. (Try to find out if the location suits your feline before you start drilling holes or sinking molly bolts.)

Make the post a controlled play center while you're at it. A few safe toys securely attached to or suspended from the post will help intrigue your pet to use it.

A company called Felix makes one of the best scratching posts around—a sturdy cedar post wrapped with rugged woven sisal and impregnated with cat-

nip that can be renewed from time to time. Cats go wild over them, and these posts can really take a beating. You can also make or buy a scratching board, rather than a post, if you're pressed for space or think your cat might prefer it. An 18 × 18-inch piece of woven sisal fiber, carpet backside out, or highly textured fabric, or even an old hemp or rope doormat can be attached to the wall beside your pet's bed or to a door or even laid out flat on the floor.

WHERE TO PUT THE POST?

Near your pet's food and water dishes is a good spot, because cats often stretch

and scratch after a good meal. Or try by the pet's bed—cats like to scratch when they wake up, too. Next to, or in front of, whatever he's been scratching would be a prime spot. Then after he gets used to using the post you can gradually move the post to where you really want it to be. Corners are a good unobtrusive place for a post, and will help assure that it never falls over. If you have a large house, more than one post might be a good investment.

POST PERSUASION

You can't assume that your pet will instantly recognize the superiority of a post for scratching purposes. You may have to help him out a little here, by spraying the post with catnip spray (available in pet shops), or rubbing and sprinkling catnip tea on it.

Stand the post on its side to start with, and gently place the cat on it to acquaint him with that nice scratchy surface. If it's a big post, put a little treat on top, or on one of the higher platforms or perches. When you catch him scratching something else, bring him over to the post and gently rub his paws on it, or (I kid you not), demonstrate the right approach by scratching a little yourself. Always praise your pet profusely when he does use the post. You might even try by training your cat to scratch the post on command (when you say a certain phrase such as "Kitty, climb") and rewarding him when he obeys.

Solution #2: Prevent

Make scratching impossible or much less likely by choice of material and design and where and how you place things. Petproofing is definitely a big part of the answer here.

In the case of furniture, wood, metal, glass, or plastic laminate won't have anything like the appeal upholstered furniture or needlepoint has for a cat. If you must have fabric, go for tightly woven fabrics with a smooth surface. And bear in mind that leather and vinyl are vulnerable and hard to repair.

Place or hang scratchable things out of reach whenever you can. Install a hook to hold imperiled drapes and curtains up out of the way when you're not home.

In doors and storm doors, see that the lower portion is solid! Damage prevention is in fact the reason so many screen and storm doors are made solid on the lower half. Or cover the whole door with a full-length mirror. And a solid sheet of wood or metal or a wooden guard can be installed over the lower third (depending on the size of your pet) of the screen panels in sliding doors.

Another form of prevention is to confine your pet, while you're gone, especially, to a room or rooms where scratchables are scarce. You can also make good use of a dog crate for this purpose.

Solution #3: Clip Those Nails

It stands to reason that it will help to trim the sharp ends of your pet's claws or nails, especially if he's an indoor pet who doesn't have a chance to have them worn down by tree bark and rough outside surfaces. Dogs, especially, will develop painful paw problems if their nails grow too long, and cats with long claws tend to scratch more often. You can cut your pet's nails yourself—take a few minutes and ask your vet to show you exactly how to do it—or you can have your vet or groomer do it.

Use clippers or nippers made especially for dogs and cats. We can't even effectively cut human toenails with a clipper made for human fingernails, so we can see that the right tool for the

purpose is important. There's a variety of good professional-quality tools available for the purpose from pet shops, livestock supply stores, and pet catalogs.

Having their nails clipped has never been very popular with pets—this is when many animals act as melodramatic as they're ever likely to get. So, if at all possible, start training your pet to accept nail clipping from puppy or kittenhood. Ease them into it gradually, clipping only one or two nails a day if necessary, so it's over with before they quite realize what happened. Praise them and give them a little treat now and then as you go along, to further encourage their cooperation. If necessary, enlist a helper to help you steady your pet at least through the initial sessions.

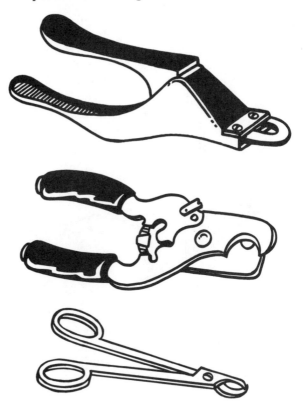

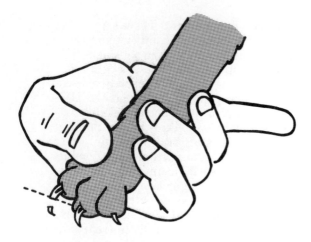

CATS

Hold the cat until he's relaxed and comfortable, then lay him on his back with his feet up. Take one paw at a time and press it gently between your thumb and forefinger to extend the claws one by one. Cut only the thin, clear, hooked end of the nail; stay at least ¼ inch away from the quick, which contains nerves and the blood vessels that nourish the nail.

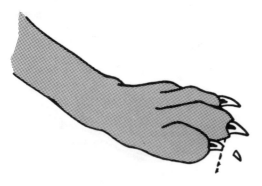

DOGS

Sit with the dog facing you on a sturdy platform or other secure surface. Pick up one paw at a time gently and cut only the tip or about the first ⅛ inch of the nail—stay away here, too, from the quick that runs about ¾ of the way down the nail. Proceed cautiously on black nails where you can't see the quick; when in doubt, cut less. If you do accidentally cut into the quick, stay calm and reassuring while you apply a styptic pencil or pressure to stop any bleeding. Be especially careful in cutting highly overgrown nails, because the quick extends out farther than in a normal nail. Trim the dewclaws—those little claws on the inside of the dog's leg—too. File the nail smooth after cutting with a file or emery board, with strokes all in the same direction, from the top of the nail downward.

How often should you snip? For dogs, clip when the toenail tips touch or clack on the floor when the dog is standing (and twice a month after that). Cats can be trimmed every two weeks, unless they habitually scratch things other than the post, in which case you should trim the front nails every week.

If you have a very touchy or clipper-shy pet, read Sherrie Lewis's excellent description of how to ease a pet into the process, in the November 1983 issue of *Dog Fancy*.

Solution #4: Training

Like other pet problem behavior, scratching can be dealt with by the behavior-changing methods outlined on page 16, including the old balloon trick—fastening balloons to the things you don't want him to scratch or climb up on. After the first few explode in his face he'll decide he'd much rather go shred toilet paper at the other end of the house. You can also construct a booby trap of noisy, scary shake cans attached to the drapes, for example. The squirt bottle can work wonders, here, too.

When the behavior you're trying to discourage involves physical damage to things, you are going to pay a certain price during the training period (in this case, a little scarred furniture). You also have to be around enough to do the training and make the correction when the act occurs.

You can cover the object the cat has been scratching with an old sheet, a plastic drop cloth, or even aluminum foil, if you can't be there to discipline him every time he tries to sink a claw. You can also cover the imperiled object with netting—cats hate to catch their claws in things. You can even tie a couple of little bells to the netting, and when you hear them ring, rush out and say "Kitty, climb," and try to maneuver him to the post. This doesn't just tell him he's done something wrong, it tells him what to do that's right. Reward and praise him when he does switch his attention to the post.

For dogs, who are prone to scratch doors when their owner leaves the house, for example, you can pretend to be leaving the house, but sneak back and listen at the door after you go out. If you hear scratching, run back in and shout "No" (and mean it). You can also throw a shake can from outside the door when you hear those little scritches.

Solution #5: Amputation

Well, that's what a lot of pet owners call it. A gentler word for it is declawing—the process of surgically removing the claw and "fingertips" of the front paws, permanently. The controversy on this subject makes the Democratic and Republican parties look like lovers. There are many who say the claws are there for a reason: to enable the cat to catch his prey and scratch to protect itself (survive!), and climb things to escape. Declawing, according to these folks, is an act right next to killing.

They say it causes more behavior problems than it solves, and there are even vets who consider the operation inhumane and refuse to do it.

Others say it's the kindest thing you can do for late twentieth century cats who must live in harmony with humans, as long as you always keep them inside, and sincerely intend to keep them as pets for the rest of their lives. I've dehorned cattle to keep them from injuring their keepers and companions, but declawing cats to control scratching does seem like a lot of change to make in a cat and a lot of money to spend to solve just one single behavior problem. If you opt for this operation, have it done before the cat is six months old, if possible—it'll be easier on his psyche and ego. Take the time to find a competent veterinary surgeon—don't be afraid to ask for references from past declawing clients—and depending where you'll live and who you go to, be prepared to spend anywhere from $50 to over $130 for the operation.

The best compromise I've heard is this: If the only way you're able, or allowed, to keep an animal is to have it declawed (rather than take it to a shelter, where its chances for a new home are slim), then consider having the operation done. If you're thinking of declawing just because it's more convenient, I'd recommend you buy a scratching post instead, trim your pet's nails regularly, and make every effort to train him not to scratch the furniture.

Chewed Up Means Clean Up

. . . and fix up, and eventually fed up! Most cats and dogs are smart enough not to chew tobacco, but everything else tasty or tooth-satisfying is fair game.

Pets will chew on plaster, pot holders, walls, door frames, electrical and phone cords, rugs, baseboards, banisters, clothes, children's toys, books, photo albums, pillows, plants, purses, belts, slippers, shoes, socks, luggage, their own beds and dishes, and the legs, arms, and edges of furniture.

The number 1 solution for curbing chewing is to provide more tempting alternatives. Pet chew-toys, many of which are impregnated with a pet-attracting scent or flavor, come in all shapes and sizes—bones or balls or rings. They divert, they're enjoyed, and they exercise the chewing instinct harmlessly. They help keep teeth clean and gums healthy, the right kind are completely safe as well as sterilizable, and they'll last forever. "The right kind" here means sturdy rawhide or hard solid rubber or the rugged nylon bones such as Nylabone. Nylabones come in flavors like ham and chocolate,

and they've been known to withstand a decade of enthusiastic chomping. There are also nylon bones like Mytibone with a little bit of real bone meal mixed in, for dogs who lack the jaw power for straight nylon, and natural bones that have been treated and sterilized to be safe and last longer.

If your pet is teething, provide him with a few ice cubes or frozen damp washcloths to ease his gum soreness and itching. Keep puppies in the chewing stage, especially, well away from household cleaners, chemicals, pesticide containers, medicines, and cigarette butts.

A chew toy needs to be the right size for your pet: a small dog won't take on too large a toy, and you don't want your big dog to be able to gnaw up his chewie in nothing flat. You may want to buy different chew toys and see which ones your pet favors before you buy a gross of anything. (You can buy chew toys in

bulk through some mail order catalogs, for example, and it will help to keep the price down.) Chew toys are cheap, when you consider that pets have managed to destroy hundreds and even thousands of dollars' worth of furnishings at a sitting. (The one-dog record is $15,000 worth in a single afternoon.)

Some training is even called for here, to underline the fact that his toys are what you want your pet to chew on. You can wiggle them around a little, pull them along on a string, or hide them, then praise and reward him for finding them. Or play a few sets of toss-and-fetch with them.

As for real bones, it's somehow a little disappointing to know that they really aren't considered good or safe for our pets. The possible exceptions are big blocky beef shank or "soup" or knuckle bones for dogs and cooked chicken necks or backs for cats. Never give a dog or cat chicken, turkey, or pork bones, or any thin or hollow bones. These can splinter and puncture an intestine, or get caught in your pet's throat and choke him.

MEDICATE!

Apply something offensive to the thing that you don't want chewed. A few bitter bites and the animal will leave it alone. There are a number of products manufactured for just this purpose, such as Chew-Guard, No Chew, Chew Stop, and others dispensed only by vets. One that works particularly well called Bitter Apple is made from crabapples and comes in a gel or spray. The gel can be used on most all sealed surfaces (it has a petroleum jelly base), but should be reapplied every day until the chewing behavior stops. The spray has an alcohol base and might stain highly polished furniture. In addition, because of its high alcohol content, it evaporates quickly and has to be reapplied more than once a day.

You can mix alum into a paste with water and spread the paste on the thing you want to protect. Or fill a spray bottle with white vinegar to anoint things like phone cords.

Hot pepper sauce also comes in handy here; brush it generously on the most recent chew target and then mist it with a little cheap diluted cologne. Your pet will come to associate the smell of the cologne with the hot taste and you can eventually fend him off with cologne alone. Some other fairly effective remedies are oil of cloves (sold in drugstores as a toothache remedy), applied with a cotton ball, and even Chinese mustard.

Most chew repellents have to be reapplied regularly, usually once a day, throughout the retraining period to keep an object effectively protected. You can even apply the repellent in front of your pet while saying "Don't touch" (or the discouraging expression of your choice) to make that bad taste a

little more educational, when and if they do encounter it.

CATCH AND CORRECT

Chewing is one of the harder bad habits to break by on-the-spot correction, since it's actually more likely to occur when you're not there. And it does no good, and even some harm, to correct a pet for chewing after the fact. He'll never be able to connect your 5 P.M. displeasure with the antimacassar he consumed early this morning. As Gwen Bohnenkamp says, "Improper correction is worse than useless. It'll just make your pet anxious, wondering what he did wrong—so he'll chew something else."

But don't let chewing go uncorrected when you do witness it. Say "No" sharply, gently disengage your pet's teeth from the object, and then hand him an acceptable chewie. Or you can say "No" followed by "Go find your toy" and keep it up until he finds one of his chew toys and latches onto it. Be sure to praise him when he does.

You can also use the spray bottle or shake can technique (see page 16).

You can "set up" a chewing correction session by bringing your pet near forbidden objects, then as he's about to lay tooth to the object, let loose with the "No," "Off" routine. You do have to be careful here to not have directly encouraged or commanded him to chew it.

A variation on this is to leave an expendable sample of a type of thing you never want chewed in a conspicuous spot, liberally doused with one of the chewing repellents mentioned earlier.

CONFINE

When you have to be away from home for hours at a stretch, you can confine your pet to a room where no chewables exist—wood furniture is something you especially don't want in there. Since it's admittedly hard to find a room that quite fits that description, confinement in a fenced yard or other safe area outdoors, or crating, is often a good solution here. Be sure to leave an appealing chew toy with your dog when you go (a little variety will be appreciated here), and it'll add that little extra something if you handle the toy a bit before you leave, to let it absorb your scent.

STIMULATE

A lot of chewing is the result of boredom and loneliness. Make sure your pet gets plenty of vigorous exercise each day— how much depends on your pet's age, size, and breed. (Check with your vet.) Letting your dog just run loose in the yard, by the way, is only considered "mild" exercise.

DESIGN

You don't want any chew toys for your pet that in any way resemble chewing contraband. Don't give your animal a pair of old sneakers to play with, then wonder why he chewed on your new running shoes. Old towels or new towels, old gloves or new gloves, scrap wood or fine furniture—they all look the same to a pet.

To help prevent the chewed shoe syndrome, store your shoes out of reach on a wire rack suspended above the bottom of the closet. (It'll also make cleaning the closet floor a snap.)

PREVENT

Pets of all kinds seem to have an irresistible attraction to electrical cords and many a pet has been badly burned or killed, and many a fire started, in the process of chewing. Pets also tug on the cords and could bring a lamp or small appliance crashing down. Heavily wrapped cords that are sturdier and at least somewhat safer can be purchased for only a little more money than the cheapies. But try to eliminate dangling cords by using suspended lighting, for example, or attaching cords to baseboards. You can also thread a cord through a curtain rod or piece of garden hose to protect it, or wrap it in aluminum foil. Protect the loose cords you can't do without with hot pepper sauce, alum paste, or vinegar.

If your pet is chewing plaster, he may need a mineral and vitamin supplement (or he may have a case of acid stomach that he's trying to treat with sheetrock antacid). Consult your vet.

And in case you're wondering, a muzzle isn't a good solution for a pet that chews. A muzzled dog will still want to chew, and the muzzle will only upset him more.

Pets Getting In the Garbage

Careless garbage handling and curious pets are the ingredients for a lot of trouble. It doesn't just get knocked over and climbed on and dug through and spread throughout the house or neighborhood, but in that garbage, amidst the savory morsels, are broken glass, cigarette butts, not quite empty containers of chemicals and poisons, sharp can lids, splintery chicken bones, and all the rest, possibly dealing you a dead pet or an expensive vet bill. Yet the solution is so simple: Don't make the garbage accessible.

If you have a pet that's strong enough to knock the garbage can over and make the lid pop off, mount the can so it can't be knocked over. Use a square can on a wood or metal strip notched to slip under the lip of the can and hold it securely. Or keep your container inside a lower cupboard or behind strong securely closing doors.

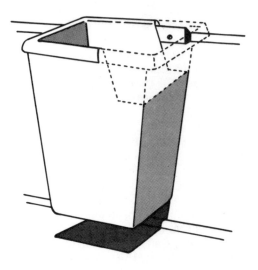

The kitchen has the most seductive garbage in the house, so be sure to use a lidded container. Garbage cans that open when you step on a pedal aren't really safe; it doesn't take long for a dog to figure out how to use it. Always wrap smelly things in plastic before dropping them in the can, and take the garbage out often, before it has a chance to develop those compelling "aged" odors. Use a small can inside in the kitchen and empty it daily into a larger can outside.

You can train your dog not to get into the garbage. Take half of a tuna fish or peanut butter sandwich and stick it under a few pieces of rolled-up newspaper in the can. Then go sit down and read a magazine. As the smell wafts over to your dog, he'll probably mosey over and put his nose in the garbage. Then you say a loud, firm "No." Or you can use a shake can, or balloons tied on top of the garbage, or put upside-down mousetraps in the garbage under a layer of paper so that when the dog touches it the trash snaps at him. You could also apply powdered alum, Bitter Apple, extra-hot mustard, or hot pepper sauce to the bag (not to any of the food in it).

When it comes to the garbage can, one reprimand or booby-trapping or shake-can session isn't going to do it—you're going to have to do it four or five times a day for two weeks. The important thing is to let the dog know he's not allowed to do this, that the garbage is a negative.

Cats can be trained, but it's slightly more difficult. A cat will wait until you're gone and then dig in, so be sure all garbage cans around cats have sturdy lids or covers. Cats don't have the weight some dogs do, so they can't step on pedals and open cans; but if you set your garbage on the counter where the dog can't get to it, the cat still can.

It's even more important, when you have pets, to disinfect and deodorize the garbage can from time to time to keep down germs and odors. To disinfect, fill the container with one ounce of Chlorasan per gallon of water and let it soak for ten to fifteen minutes. Add a squirt of water-soluble deodorizer (like Nilodor Surface Deodorizer) to the disinfec-

tant solution for super-effective odor control. Use a nylon scrubbing sponge, a toilet brush, or other long-handled brush to scrub it out. Rinse it well and sun-dry if possible. I'd let a last squirt or two of Chlorasan solution dry on the can to retard bacteria growth.

Outside

Outside, store your garbage in metal or hard plastic cans with tight-fitting lids. The most durable are heavy-duty molded plastic cans such as Rubbermaid Brutes or Continental Huskees, available at janitorial supply stores in 30- or 44-gallon sizes. They'll outlast a metal can many times over, are quieter than metal, and are even available with casters.

The biggest single cleanup problem is that of pets tipping over and spilling the garbage, so get a can with a heavy tight-fitting lid that will stay on even if the can tips over. You can weigh down the lid with a big rock, or bricks, but it's

still susceptible to knockover; better are the quick-release locking straps available for the garbage can, or elastic bungee cords with metal hooks on the ends.

Put a sturdy five- or six-foot wire fence or enclosure around the garbage area, with a gate. Or if you don't enclose them, suspend or mount your outside garbage cans. A lot of mess and spills can be avoided if animals can't tip the can over or unseat the lid. You could mount them against the house, to a wood deck, on a post or pole, on a sturdy fence, etc.

If your municipality requires you to put out garbage in disposable bags rather than closed cans, you can try one of the commercial pet repellent sprays on the bags to keep pets away. It's also worth the investment to buy extra thick or super-strength bags or even double-bag your garbage, if it has to sit outside until pickup day. Nothing attracts rats and mice faster than free food and you don't want them outside your house feasting and reproducing.

Dragging In Unmentionables

You can't believe—or can you?—the size and variety and condition of things a pet can bring home. Our dog once dragged in the complete head and hide of a 4-point buck from a distant neighbor's farm. Dogs always enjoy the freshness of a mess out in the open, then bring it home to you when it's rank and fly-infested. And a cat will sit there and expect you to enjoy its proud offering, or devour a live meal in the middle of the living room. What to do with the pet in such a case is definitely second to what to do with the "whatever."

To get rid of the stuff your pet has

dragged in, get a plastic bag and turn it inside out, then put your hand in it and use it like a glove to pick up the mess. Turn the bag right side out again, tie up the top securely, and throw it away. If you don't even want to touch it through a plastic bag, scoop it into a small box or paper bag with a couple of pieces of cardboard. Then put the whole mess in a plastic trash bag and take it to the trash disposal area immediately. This will seal off odor and reduce the chance of it being dragged off again. If you're left with a lingering odor, treat the area with bacteria/enzyme solution, and it may not be a bad idea to apply some Chlorasan solution to the area of a particularly messy pickup. (If you want to

disinfect *and* deodorize here, be sure to use the bacteria/enzyme product first and give it time to work before applying any disinfectant.)

Be sure to wash your hands well after drag-in cleanup duty. Rodents and rabbits and the like carry diseases that can be transmitted to humans. (A pregnant woman should recruit someone else to do this particular cleanup chore, or if she has no choice but do it herself, she should wear rubber gloves to avoid any risk of toxoplasmosis.)

What do you do if your pet brings in a critter that's still alive? *Don't* try to pry the animal away from your pet—your pet may scratch or even bite you to keep from losing his trophy. Try to startle

your pet into dropping it (dropping a shake can next to him might do the trick). If he does drop it, put him outside or confine him to another room to keep him from snatching up the wounded animal again. The next step is really a judgment call. You can either try to collect the animal yourself to take to a vet, or call someone else (like your city's Animal Control Department) to come take care of it. Try not to pick up a hurt animal with your bare hands, since it might still have the strength to bite you. You also don't want to put a stunned wild animal inside your car to take him to get help, because he can wake up and go berserk while you're trying to drive. And hopefully your pet has already had his rabies vaccination, since many wild animals can pass on the disease.

Prevention

Training has a place here, though it poses some special problems. Let's say your dog finds a dead possum and tries to bring it into the yard, so you tell him no and he stops. If he doesn't find another dead thing for a couple of weeks or months, he won't remember what you told him last time because there's no continuity in the training. But if your animal finds or kills things and brings them home regularly, it's easy to train him because he gets day-after-day training, and thus continuity.

You can bell a cat to sabotage his hunting, though some cats do learn to time their leaps to account for the bell. If you do put a bell on your cat, make sure it's on a breakaway collar. And fencing can certainly help here. Dogs and cats can't drag large things over a fence, or through it, and if they're kept in a fenced yard they can't get out to get "it" in the first place.

MUNCH!
MUNCH!

Pets Eating Houseplants

Life is funny. We coax, tempt, and bribe our kids for years to get them to eat their vegetables, and our pet, who has no apparent reason to consume anything green does so of his own free will, enthusiastically. But houseplants actually pose a greater threat of poisoning to cats than household chemicals; not a few of the exotic species of plants we keep to cheer our interiors are poisonous to animals in whole or part.

Cats actually do have their reasons for chomping on the caladiums, which range from the desire for a little roughage or green tonic to the need to vomit up a hairball (they somehow know that eating grass or other greenery will bring on the heaves). Here are some ideas to keep your plants intact, give your pet some healthier eating habits, and make it easier on the cleaner.

1. **Grow your cat his own pot of greens.** *There are prepackaged and preplanted kitty grazing gardens available, or you can just plant a little pot of lawn seed mix, wheat, rye, oat grass, alfalfa, or even parsley.*

2. **Add some safe greenery** *to your pet's diet. Cats are carnivores, but some enjoy a chance to eat vegetables and even fruits. Add a little chopped raw or cooked green vegetables to his food.*

3. **Make your plants inaccessible,** *which generally means hang them. (If a cat wants to get on the highest, narrowest shelf, he'll do it, and once up there, the cat isn't what falls off.) Hang plants somewhere that can't be reached by a flying leap, or from a cat perch a neck-stretch away. For plants too heavy to hang, put chicken wire around the base so the cats can't get to the pot but you can still water it through the wire.*

4. **Choosing heavy pots** *for your houseplants will lessen the likelihood of knockdowns. And covering the entire surface of the exposed soil with decorative rocks or brown needlepoint canvas will discourage "litter box" excavations. You can also lay down a protective barrier of aluminum foil in front of your plants—cats don't like to walk on it.*

    Avoid mulches such as shredded bark that make great playbait. Also try to avoid the most pet-tempting plants such as plants with frilly or feathery foliage (house palms, ferns), etc. Check with your fellow cat fanciers as to what plants seem to have a fatal attraction for felines.

5. **Train your pet away** *from your plants with a sharp loud "No!" and a handclap or the old squirt bottle (you can mist your plants while you're at it, too). For extreme cases, remove all your houseplants from sight except one luscious specimen. Then coat the bottoms of the leaves of that plant with hot pepper sauce and mist or sponge the tops of the leaves with a solution of cheap cologne, diluted to one part cologne to five parts water.*

    Then make sure your cat notices the rigged plant. Plunk it down in the middle of the floor and call your cat over to it and waggle the branches around a little. After he nibbles on the plant and tastes the pepper, he'll probably sprint for the water dish. And he'll associate the smell of the cologne with the sting of the hot pepper. Move the peppered plant to different locations in the house and freshen up the pepper sauce and cologne from time to time. Soon you only have to mist this plant (or any of your plants) with diluted cologne to keep your pet away from it—he'll think the hot pepper is still there. All the while that you're discouraging him from your plants with the hot pepper technique, encourage him to chew on his greens.

    A variation on this technique is to use a five to one solution of water and eucalyptus oil instead of the cologne, or to sprinkle powdered ginger on the tips of the most accessible leaves of your plants, misting the leaves first to help the powder adhere.

6. **A pitched-over houseplant** *can be vacuumed up, after you've scooped up the bulk of the mess with your dustpan and squeegee. If any dirt stains remain after vacuuming, give them a little squirt of all-purpose cleaning solution. Wait a minute or two to let the chemicals work to release the solids from the surface, and then you can blot them up easily.*

Don't use systemic insecticides if you have a houseplant-prone pet. It'll only multiply the poisoning possibilities. And if your cat does manage to consume a plant and is showing signs of intense distress or poisoning, you can call the University of Illinois Toxicology Hotline for Animals seven days a week: (217) 333-3611. Or rush him to the vet along with a sample of the plant he ate.

Pets Drooling All Over

Many of the hundreds of media broadcasts I do a year are call-ins, where listeners call and pose their cleaning problems. Rarely have I been stumped entirely, but a pet owner who called KMOX in St. Louis finally did it.

"Mr. Aslett, I have two boxers, and they have a tendency to drool a bit—like by the bucketful. When they shake their heads they shower the walls, furniture, windows, and any people passing. How do I clean off all those glistening dried droplets?"

I had no idea that dogs could drool enough to cause a cleaning problem. But heavy-duty drooling in pets is a reality, and if you happen to own a boxer, bloodhound, mastiff, bulldog, Saint Bernard, or other breed with a "pendulous lip," it's more than a reality, it's a river! One pet owner offered the profound solution, "Wipe off their jaws frequently," and a frustrated chow owner suggested, "Put a bib on 'em!"

If it weren't for drooling by old Pavlov's pooches we'd never have known about conditioned responses—the key to a lot of animal and human behavior and training. Preventing conditioned response, in fact, is one way to cure at least some of the drooling. Hunger and anticipation of food is one big reason for drooling, especially when we get in the habit of feeding animals around the table. They start drooling the minute they hear that fork clink on the plate. If you train your pet to keep strictly away from the table (or even out of the room) and all its food stimulus before and in between meals, that alone will eliminate a lot of drooling.

Cats drool, too, often when they're feeling especially happy, such as when they're being petted. If you can't stand your cat kneading and drooling on you, about the only thing you can do is to avoid lap-sitting and heavy petting.

A drooling animal who normally doesn't drool should be checked by a vet. Abnormal drooling could be caused by a number of things, such as poisoning, a medicine the animal is taking, nervousness, overheating, a respiratory disease, or a gum or tooth problem.

As for cleanup, a solution of all-purpose neutral cleaner in warm water is the best way to remove saliva when fresh. Hardened, dried saliva doesn't come off surfaces instantly or easily, and a strong degreaser may be called for to get the deposits up. Wet the spot down with the cleaning solution and leave it on for a few minutes before you wipe it off.

The enzymes in saliva can react with light, causing the droplets to darken as they dry. If there is staining, blot the area carefully with a hydrogen peroxide-wetted cloth, but be sure to test this first in an inconspicuous area.

If the saliva deposits are on a porous surface such as upholstery or carpeting, you might want to give the area a couple of quick sprays of Chlorasan solution after cleaning and just let it dry there, to prevent bacterial growth.

Pets "Scooting" on the Floor or Carpet

If you catch your cat or dog "scooting" around on the carpet on its rear end, he's not protesting the lack of toilet paper in the litter box. This kind of behavior, while sometimes a sign of worms, more often than not means anal gland impaction. Dogs and cats both have glands on either side of the anus which excrete a scent when they defecate, as a territorial marking device.

When these glands fail to function properly, they become impacted and uncomfortable, and the animal will scoot its rear end on the floor or ground in an attempt to clear them. It may also lick the rectal area or bite its tail. Anal gland secretions can have a very strong unpleasant odor, especially when the glands are infected or inflamed.

The vet or dog groomer will usually squeeze the glands to empty them during your pet's regular visits, and this may be all that's needed. If the glands are infected, treatment with an antibi-otic is usually called for, and in cases of chronic impaction, the glands can be surgically removed. Spayed animals don't have as much of a problem with anal gland impaction, and cats suffer less from this than do dogs. It's a very common problem with unneutered male dogs.

For the sake of your pet's good health, and that of the human household members (impacted anal glands can harbor strep germs, for example) as well as your own comfort and the cleanliness of your home, don't let an anal gland problem continue untreated. Consult your vet as as soon as you notice the problem. And if you do get anal gland secretions on your carpeting, floors, or bedspread, clean and deodorize the spot the same way you would the infamous #2 (see page 67). This basically means treat the spot with Nilotex, or if it's become an embedded odor problem, with bacteria/enzyme digester.

The Heat is On

Legendary people in powerful leadership positions have been known to destroy cities and pillage entire continents for love, so why should it be different for pets? An unspayed female would much rather listen to what her sex drive has to say, than to you.

A female dog's first heat usually appears when she's between the age of six

and twelve months. After that, she'll come into heat twice a year, with each heat period lasting for two to three weeks. During this time her vulva will swell noticeably and begin to discharge a small amount of blood. Blood is one of the harder stains to remove, and she'll be leaving little spots of it all over the house, and all over the furniture, if she's allowed to jump up there. The heat period also causes a bitch to urinate much more often than normal. If you leave her home alone all day, she may not be able to hold herself until you return. A female dog, eager to mate but unable to get outside, may also try to escape by scratching at doors and floors. Some females experience a "false pregnancy" and try to build a nest by digging a hole in or tearing up pillows, beds, or sofa cushions.

The following are some ideas to keep the mess and damage down (and keep your pet from getting pregnant):

- *Have her spayed—the* best *solution of all!*

- *Confine her to an easy-to-clean area of the house, a securely closed garage or reliably fenced yard, or a crate.*

- *Keep her inside all day and watch her like a hawk (or walk her only on a short leash, accompanied by a bodyguard).*

- *Put her in a boarding kennel until her period is over (and shell out beaucoup bucks for it, most likely).*

- *Cover any furniture you do allow her on with plastic or an old sheet.*

- *Get some doggy birth control pills from your vet. Most of the ones presently available have to be fed to a dog every day, to prevent her from coming into heat.*

- *You can buy chlorophyll pills for her to eat or use anti-mating sprays to try to cover up her mating scent, but like brewer's yeast and cedar oil for fleas, nobody can say for sure whether they really work or not—you pay your money and take your chances.*

- *Buy her a few pair of doggy sanitary pants or pads to absorb the blood. These can be uncomfortable for your dog because they hold bacteria in close to the body and keep the area moist, often causing chafing or a rash much like diaper rash. Use them only as a last resort.*

- *Keep your cleaning arsenal handy— bacteria/enzyme digester and a pet stain remover.*

A female cat becomes sexually mature anywhere between six and eight months, and may come into heat two or three more times a year after that. She usually won't cause as much mess as a dog because she's smaller and doesn't discharge blood, though she can still cause damage by her frantic rolling, rubbing, and lunging, and by such things as tearing holes in the screen door to get outside. And the yowling of a female cat in heat is enough to set your teeth on edge. Once again, the best solution is spaying.

Lassie Wants You to Come Home

Pets become very attached to their human families. When you leave, your pet isn't at all sure you'll ever be back. Coping with destructive behavior caused by what the pet experts call "separation anxiety" calls for the same concern and understanding you'd use with a child.

Dogs are descended from animals that live in family groups, or packs, whose members spend three quarters or more of their time together, so staying all alone is alien to them. In the animal world, if your pack leaves you behind it's because you're diseased, dying, or unwanted. So your pet thinks he has leprosy and actually you're just going to work.

Dogs that have come from a shelter or had previous owners are more likely to suffer separation anxiety, because they really do know what it is to be abandoned, and they live in constant fear of that happening again.

When a dog gets anxious he'll nibble on this and chew on that, and anxiety also increases the possibility of accidents in the house. He may also lose his appetite and get depressed.

Punishment is completely off the point here. To reduce destructive behavior brought on by separation anxiety we have to reduce our pet's anxiety by gradually accustoming him to being alone. There's an excellent pamphlet, *The Dog That Cannot Be Left Alone* (you

can get a copy by writing to Gaines Booklets, P.O. Box 8177, Kankakee, Illinois, 60902) devoted solely to this subject, but here's a quick review of the kind of training you have to do.

- *Start with short absences the dog can tolerate, for example ten seconds.*

- *Remain calm and quiet as you come and go, no wild or enthusiastic greetings.*

- *Repeat until you're sure the animal is not anxious, then gradually increase the length of your absence. If the animal backslides, then practice more short absences.*

- *Next practice being gone for different lengths of time so the dog can't anticipate exactly when you'll return. After he's used to you being gone an hour or more, he'll gradually learn to tolerate longer intervals.*

Don't let your pet bowl you over when you come in. Greet him quietly, keep excitement to a minimum, and save the play for later. The less fuss you make over coming and going, the less anxiety-producing your absences will be. Wild hellos get a dog so keyed up for your return that he may turn to destructive behavior if you're delayed.

A whiney anxious good-bye from you also signals the animal that something is wrong and leaves him to wonder about it all day. So if you find yourself saying "Now good-bye, sweetheart, be a good dog and don't eat Mommy's shoes—please, please be good," you may be part of the problem. Instead, calmly say "Good-bye," toss him a toy, and go!

When you're home, have your pet stay alone in a room for at least some small part of the day. A puppy shut in alone for his nap every day, for example, will learn to accept it. It will also help this particular problem if you discourage your pet from being in constant contact with you: always sitting on your lap, sleeping with you, etc. This will help him be less dependent on you.

Confinement

It's a good idea to confine a pet left alone to a certain part of the house, and "pet-proof" the area: make sure there's nothing he can harm and nothing that can harm him in there.

You want the room to be large enough that he can get some exercise (exactly how big depends on the size of the animal). A vinyl or tile floor is a much better idea than a carpeted one, but be sure to put his bed in there or some washable rugs or blankets to lay on. If at all possible go for a sunlit room with a window, and leave it open a crack so he can catch a whiff of what's going on outside. Remove any furniture that can't stand a little chewing or be slept on by your pet.

You don't want a room packed with your prize possessions. Remove or protect anything that's hopelessly attached to your heartstrings. The emotional expense of Rover consuming the last handmade tapestry Great-Grandmother Ethel ever made will be much greater than the few dollars or hours you spend pet-proofing the canine suite. (No matter how grateful your spouse may be to finally be rid of that moth-eaten tapestry.)

If you have a dog or a cat that consistently causes problems while you're away, you might consider crate-training him. Dogs may even draw a margin of comfort from being in their crate when they're left alone. But it's important to gradually accustom your pet to being in the crate, or a crate will only worsen the problem. For directions as to exactly how to do this, write to Gwen Bohnenkamp, Animal Behavior Dept.,

San Francisco SPCA, 2500 16th Street, San Francisco, California, 94103, and ask for her booklet on separation anxiety. (A tax-deductible donation to the SF SPCA will be appreciated.)

Boredom is the major threat to your pet's good behavior. Toys and "acceptable chewies" offer your pet entertainment when you're gone. Be sure to rotate toys and chewies every few days so they're new and exciting to your pet. And put your pet's toys away when you come home. Save them for the lonely times. Keep a favorite toy by the door and toss it to your pet as you go. If you rub it in your palms he'll be doubly drawn to it by your scent.

If something frightens your animal, he can do a lot of damage alone in your home. Music can help to soothe the anxious beast, and for that matter the lonely, howling beast. It also muffles outside noises like horns and sirens and shrieking kids. A radio playing makes a good companion for your dog. Tune in a station with more human chatter than music, as he's more interested in a human voice. A long-playing recording of your voice might serve even better.

Exercise and Obedience Training

Our pets react to boredom in a way we often do—sleep is the primary occupation of the average pet when the master is away. So when you get home your pet has a store of pent-up energy ready for release the minute you walk in the door.

Exercise your pet in the morning just before you leave, again when you get home, and before he goes to bed. He deserves special care and attention when the family does arrive home. Exercise, walks, and obedience training will help him cope with your daily absences. To

quote *Dog Fancy:* "Trained dogs even *look* less bored; perhaps it's because they have something to look forward to at the end of the day. Twenty or thirty minutes a day in a one-on-one session with you gives your dog quality time to perform all the things he's learned and be praised by you. The security he derives from this will help carry him through the long day without resorting to destructive behavior."

Ideally your pet should be let out at least once during the day to relieve himself. If you can't make it home then consider a "pet sitter" service or a nearby neighbor willing to take this on. A daily visit with your pet might be a welcome break in the day for a retired or elderly person. Or a petless child might love to take him for a walk after school. Your pet's food and water and toilet needs can be tended and at the same time a little companionship will interrupt an otherwise lonely day.

Professional pet sitters are popping up all over the country. They feed, water, exercise, and even administer medication to pets. They will either come to your home or have you bring your pet to them. The right sitter can alleviate a lot of potential mess for you.

In our latchkey society imagine the number of pets home alone with children after school. If a pet alone can make a mess, add a kid or two to the recipe and see what cooks up. Kids sharing snacks with Fido; six feet instead of two tracking mud in the back door—the possibilities are endless. Establishing some rules here will help keep cleaning down. And be careful, when chastising a child for a co-made mess, that the child doesn't dole out some punishment of his own on the animal when left alone with it.

Some undesirable behavior may be the result of a simple case of hunger. Although adult dogs may only need to be fed once a day, left alone all day with little to do and an empty stomach, the rattan rocking chair might get to looking pretty appetizing. A solution for some cases of destructive chewing is to feed your pet a light meal early in the morning, and take him out twenty or thirty minutes later. Then give him another light meal in the evening when you return.

GET YOUR PET A PET

It's often just as easy to care for two pets as one, and another dog or cat can keep your pet entertained and happy while you're gone all day. If your pet is a pup, an older companion is the best idea, as two puppies can get into twice as much trouble. And be sure pet pals are neutered so they don't create a whole litterful of entertainment. Even a bird, well out of reach in a cage, can be a welcome diversion for your dog.

If you have a cat and bring home another one, keep them separated from each other for a few days to a week, then let the new pet come in and meet the old one. Don't make a fuss over the new pet; instead, give your old pet more attention to help reduce any jealousy he might feel. This also applies if you bring home a dog when you have a cat, if you have a dog and get another one, or if you have a dog and bring home a cat.

The following combinations are generally the best recipe for pet peace and harmony: kitten and puppy; two kittens; mature, neutered cat and puppy or kitten; two mature, neutered cats (two females or a male and a female).

PAY ATTENTION TO HIM

You can go to great lengths to enrich your pet's life, with toys, pet buddies, etc., but remember that in the end it's *you*, the master, who makes the big difference. As Gwen Bohnenkamp says: "Remember, your pet can't build model airplanes, learn Italian, or shoot pool when you're not home. So when you are, set aside some time to give him undivided attention."

Don't try to discipline your pet when you get home for accidents or damage that occurred while you were gone. It does no good to punish at 5 P.M. for an act that occurred at 10 A.M.—he's forgotten all about it. It will only confuse him and give him negative associations with your homecoming that may cause him to perform other forbidden acts while fretting about it. Nor in this case will it do any good to wait outside until the dog performs an unwanted behavior, then rush in and scold him. Punishment just isn't an effective way to treat separation anxiety. And it'll only compound any guilty feelings you may have about leaving him alone all day.

Are Pets Worth Cleaning Up After?

Next time you're patting yourself on the back for all you do for your pet, including cleaning up after it, the next time a tiny tendril of doubt creeps in and you're wondering if the pet is worth the mess, remember a couple of things. You've had the same thoughts about your kids a few times, your marriage, your school, your job. For all the money those pets cost, all the worry they can cause, all the trips to the vet and shattered nerves when a car screeches out on the street, those little creatures do more than a little to better our life quality, and give us a few gifts that nothing can replace.

Although the bottom line of life is to be loved, we humans work hard to not have that happen to us. We become obsessed with ambition and success, and cut off from our fellow humans, or lazy, selfish, and undisciplined (all the very qualities that tend to reduce our chances of loving and being loved). Our parents let us do it, our friends let us do it, our kids let us do it, the government lets us get away with it . . .

But pets won't! If we take from them, we have to give back—with the caress we get some mess, which we can't leave or forget about like we can and do so many things. Pets won't let us be ungrateful.

The next time you get disgusted with the dog dish, a little lethargic about the litter box, stop and think about what we get in return for this price of a little pet cleaning. The facts are proven (in clinical tests, even, if you please). Pets are:

- *Good company*
- *Fun*
- *An encouragement to exercise*
- *Good healthy exercise for our emotions, too*
- *A bit of nature we can enjoy in even the most crowded city*
- *A help in organizing our schedules and our lives*
- *Promoters of self-esteem and confidence in us, their owners*
- *Vivid instruction in the art of caretaking*
- *An opportunity to observe and adjust to the realities of life and death*
- *An aid and catalyst in human relationships, even marriage*
- *Mental and even physical salvation for thousands of people (the blind, hearing impaired, mentally ill, etc.)*
- *Protectors of our property*
- *Pest exterminators*
- *An aid in crime prevention and law enforcement*

They save us from loneliness and take our minds off our troubles—and for all this they get no regular pay or benefits, bonuses, vacations, just a few morsels of food and a few minutes of care a day. Now that's a deal if I ever heard one!

The chemistry of pets and people has delighted mankind for centuries and it can't be measured by the cost of flea collars or eroded by a midnight bark or meow or two. Pets make our lives a lot richer and we owners get a lot for a little cleaning—we get total unquestioning love, absolute loyalty, and a pattern of forgiveness no Christian has yet perfected. Anything that would do all this for us and a hundred times more, is certainly worth getting out the scrub brush for on occasion.

Pets are . . . an antidote to the mental poisons of an urban environment. If they don't fit in this environment, then neither do we, for we are all animals together.

—The Handbook of Animal Welfare

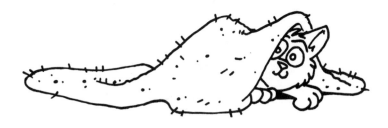

A word of thanks . . .

Everyone who reads a good book stops somewhere and says "Wow, this author sure knows a lot, how did he ever get all this material together?"

You can bet I didn't sit in a lakeside cabin in Alaska for a few months and suddenly show up unshaven with a 200-page polished manuscript solving one of society's big problems—pet mess. I've had lots of real-life experience with the subject, and firsthand knowledge of the need for the book, but I was only the driver of the project. A team of tireless huskies pulled it through:

Carol Cartaino—Our lead dog, who came up with the original idea for the book and edited and art directed it, as well as spearheaded the research on the whole project.

Steve Medellin—Pet enthusiast, word processor wizard, and a fine man at the phone when it comes to eliciting and recording information from all those other experts out there.

Robert Betty—The artist full of animal imagination who brought all our pet dilemmas to life in these pages.

Laura Simons—Editorial resource person, who chased down the answers to all those nagging little questions and was an invaluable help with the pet-proofing portions of the book.

Mark Browning—President of Varsity of Texas and master of practical reality, who found the time in his very busy schedule to help us compile the technical information herein.

Arlo, Jackie, and *Jana Luke*, who lent us their cleaning knowhow, pet owner's perspective, and well-executed general assistance, respectively.

Tobi Haynes, who contributed her considerable information-assimilating and wordcrafting skills to the effort, when they were most needed.

Skip Berry, *Beth Racine*, *George Wagner*, *Tracy Monroe*, and *Susan Herrmann*, who helped us ferret out the pet wisdom of the ages (or at least the latter twentieth century).

Nancy Everson—My operations manager, who managed and arranged things and smoothed the way, and kept the doubts and worries at bay.

And finally, *the Animals of the Ross Park Zoo* of Pocatello, for their endless inspiration and understanding.

130

Index

About the Author

Don Aslett is an energetic and successful businessman, author, entertainer, and consultant who has been called the world's #1 cleaning expert.

Don had a rural background, so his childhood luckily was filled with the companionship and responsibility of numerous pets and animals. "Feed your animals before you eat," "Never leave an animal without clean bedding," "Take care of an overheated animal before you worry about your own sunburn or sore feet" were the kinds of rules Don was raised by. As a college student he started to clean for friends and neighbors to earn his way through school. This "college job" operation, Varsity Contractors, Inc., has grown into one of the nation's leading professional cleaning companies and Don has become a true leader of the industry.

In thirty years of professional cleaning, he and his company have cleaned thousands and thousands of pet households. In the course of writing several best-selling books on cleaning and making more than 2,500 TV, radio, and media appearances, he also listened to thousands of questions about cleaning up after pets around the house. He knew this book was needed—and a natural.

Learn more about how to save housecleaning time and money with these other bestselling books and video by Don Aslett:

Is There Life After Housework? Shows you step by step how to clean like the professional do. 192 pages/$8.95

Don Aslett's Video Seminar: Is There Life After Housework? 95 minutes of action-packed cleaning instruction. $29.95 (VHS)

Do I Dust or Vacuum First? Answers the 100 most-often-asked housecleaning questions. 183 pages/$7.95

Clutter's Last Stand Learn how to get rid of clutter–once and for all. 276 pages/$9.95

Make Your House Do the Housework Hundreds of exciting ways to redecorate or design cleaning and maintenance out of your home. 202 pages/$9.95

Who Says It's a Woman's Job to Clean? Aslett gets men to start doing their share of the housework! 122 pages/$5.95

These books make great gifts for weddings, showers, or any special occasion, so use this coupon to order your copies today!